The Louise Noun Collection

Art by Women

Edited by

Jo-Ann Conklin

The University of Iowa Museum of Art

Published by The University of Iowa Museum of Art
on the occasion of the exhibition "The Louise Noun
Collection: Art by Women"

The University of Iowa Museum of Art
March 24 through May 13, 1990

The Des Moines Art Center
May 25 through August 5, 1990

Production of this catalogue was made possible by the
support of the following generous contributors:

Elizabeth Ballantine and Paul Leavitt
Linda and Douglas Behrendt
Louise A. Blosten
Ellen and John Buchanan
Kay and Matthew Bucksbaum
Melva and Martin Bucksbaum
Robert M. and Pat A. Donhowe
Karlen and Robert Fellows
Bruce J. Gantz
Mary K. Gantz
Antonia Hamilton
Iowa State Bank and Trust Company
Dan Johnston
Matilda A. Jung
Eunice Kuyper
Harriette and Robert Lubetkin
Mary Keough Lyman and Herbert Lyman
Joan and Robert E. Mannheimer
Nexus Breakfast Club
Louise Noun
Peggy Patrick
Paul A. and Stacy Polydoran
Louise and Watson Powell, Jr.
Joseph Rosenfield
Dorothy Schramm
Frank and Nancy Seiberling
Mary Louise Smith
Dr. and Mrs. Jack Spevak
Joyce and W. Richard Summerwill
Richard M. and Buffie P. Tucker
Helen J. Urban
Mrs. Rudolph W. Weitz
Shirley and Darrell Wyrick

Cover: Olga Rozanova. *Directional Lines,* 1913.
Oil on canvas, 39⅜ × 31 (100.0 × 78.7).

Photo credits: All photographs by Mark Tade except Bishop,
Women Walking, no. 1, Höch, *Circling Forms,* Klien, *Tower Caving
In,* by David Penney, Des Moines; Exter, *Composition,* courtesy
Annely Juda Fine Art; Greene, *Construction in Grey and Black,*
courtesy Washburn Gallery, New York; Krasner, *Black and White
Collage,* courtesy Robert Miller Gallery, New York; Pelton,
Ecstasy, courtesy Robert York Gallery, New York; Prina,
Composition, 1941, and *Composition,* 1943, courtesy Galerie
Gmurzynska, Cologne.

Design:	David Stone
Typesetting:	Annie Graham Publishing Services, Iowa City, Iowa
Printing:	Pepco, Cedar Rapids, Iowa

Contents

Foreword and Acknowledgments

Louise Noun is one of those truly exceptional people who are fundamental to the social and intellectual landscape of our state. Ms. Noun is a woman of two abiding passions, the arts and progressive social activism, and she has long sought to explore their mutual relationship. Her interest in the arts was encouraged by her mother and formalized in her studies at Radcliffe College, where she earned a master's degree in art history and museum management. Her collecting of art by women, though, began in earnest in the early 1960s, while she was working on *Strong-Minded Women,* her account of the women's suffrage movement in Iowa (published in 1969 by the Iowa State University Press). It was then that her sensitivity to and identification with the gender-based adversity suffered by many women artists came to the fore. As this exhibition and its catalogue attest, Ms. Noun has collected remarkable objects. With the diligence so characteristic of her, she began to learn *about* the remarkable women who had produced the paintings she collected, and, more important, she began to learn *from* their lives. The seriousness of her collecting is reflected in her expert knowledge about particular women artists and in her connoisseurship. It is also seen in the ways that collecting and knowing about art and artists inform Ms. Noun's social advocacy and activism. She was a founding member of Iowa's chapter of the National Organization for Women.

The exhibition of Louise Noun's collection is a memorable event for several reasons. For one, it documents a particular sensitivity and series of choices, and it illustrates how an individual important to the recent history of Iowa has lived a long and useful life. For another, many of the works Ms. Noun has chosen to collect are by artists about whom we know little and whose genius is just beginning to be recognized. Neglect of these women artists is due to the sorts of gender bias against which Ms. Noun has long struggled. In her collection and in this exhibition she wins a significant victory in making this work and the rich lives it represents available to a wide public.

We at The University of Iowa Museum of Art celebrate the exhibition of Ms. Noun's collection for several reasons beyond these. As part of our exhibition program, we will present prints, drawings, and paintings by Hannah Höch, Gabriele Münter, and other women artists represented in our permanent collections. The presence of the Noun Collection puts these works into context, sets them off, complements them, and provokes a variety of comparisons with them. The juxtapositions possible between the Noun Collection and our permanent collections allow us to learn and teach a great deal. This process will be enhanced by a symposium and other activities that will bring together scholars, students, collectors, and other art enthusiasts from across our campus, region, and state, to discuss the works and lives of the artists of our exhibition.

But again, the stimulus for these rewarding activities is the Noun Collection. Louise Noun has collected art following her passions and her personal connoisseurship, and the cohesiveness of her collection helps us better to understand the impact of art on an individual's life. An exhibition of one collector's treasures provides an unusual opportunity to rediscover that art itself is emotion and sensitivity, giving and stating, defiance and communication, beauty and awareness.

"The Louise Noun Collection" has been a collaborative effort from the start, and an immensely enjoyable experience. I wish to extend my sincere thanks to all those who have participated. The exhibition opens at the UIMA and travels to the Des Moines Art Center. We look forward to enhancing this fruitful collaboration between our two institutions. Friends of Louise Noun from around the state, and especially in Des Moines and Iowa City, have demonstrated their belief in the principles for which Ms. Noun stands. Through their generous financial contributions, they have helped us to celebrate some of Ms. Noun's many accomplishments. Darrell Wyrick and Antonia Hamilton of The University of Iowa Foundation have in many ways informed people across Iowa of our exhibition program, while making many enduring friends for The University of Iowa Museum of Art. Our catalogue authors have been diligent and innovative, and it has been a pleasure to work with them. My thanks to the many artists, gallery owners and staff, and members of other organizations providing our researchers with information about the artists of Ms. Noun's collection. Thanks, too, to Martha Chamallas, professor of law and chair of the Women's Studies Program, and to Professor of History Linda Kerber, the May Brodbeck Professor in Liberal Arts and also a member of the Women's Studies Program; to the staff of The University of Iowa Translation Laboratory; and to the many other individuals and institutions on campus that have offered us their support.

Most especially, I wish to recognize the staff of The University of Iowa Museum of Art who have worked so hard to make this exhibition program an aesthetic and intellectual success. Jo-Ann Conklin has ably assisted me from the beginning of this project, bearing primary responsibility for the implementation of this exhibition. I owe a special measure of appreciation to her. Members of Jo-Ann's editorial and research team include Gail Zlatnik and Erin Barnes. My thanks to David Stone for graphic design and Mark Tade for photography; Jane Ju and Jane Stone for arranging the symposium and educational materials; Mary MacGregor and Martha Yoder for organizing an exhibition of works on paper from our permanent collection to complement the Noun Collection; Jeff Martin for registration; Dave Dennis, Jim Lindell, and the technical crew for exhibition design and coordination; and, as always, Jo Jones and Betty Breazeale for keeping the office going and the ship afloat. It is a sincere pleasure to be part of this team.

Mary H. Kujawski
Director

Introduction

In the beginning . . . sort of:
An Anecdote

One afternoon nearly fifteen years ago, I received a telephone call from a friend in Los Angeles who was the curator of a private collection. She was inquiring whether the Des Moines Art Center—of which I was director at the time—would be interested in borrowing a painting by the Russian artist Natalia Gontcharova. The curator explained that she had been instrumental in locating the work at a gallery in Paris, from which it had been purchased. She described it with mounting enthusiasm, comparing it favorably to works by Kandinsky, Konchalovsky, and Larionov (Gontcharova's husband) which the museum had exhibited previously from that same collection. She stated that the Gontcharova would shortly be en route from the collector's apartment in New York to his home in California and that it could easily stay in Iowa for several months if I were so inclined. Since the possibility, then as now, of seeing important works by the Russian avant-garde in this country is severely limited, I readily agreed.

When the painting arrived, I was struck by its beauty and its power. Painted in the artist's Neoprimitivist style with fauvist colors and expressive lines, the solid peasant forms exuded dignity and strength. It was truly a museum painting in every way, one that would be popular with the general public as well as with connoisseurs.

But even before the painting could be installed in the museum's galleries, another phone call came from the curator in California. She was obviously agitated, for she had just learned that the recently acquired Gontcharova had been banished from the collector's New York apartment by his even more recently acquired second wife. Furthermore, the latter had been insistent that the painting be sold, for she did not wish to see it in California either; it had something to do with the colors in the picture. The curator was beside herself, I was amused, and we both were flabbergasted by this turn of events.

Since the painting had now become available for purchase, might not the museum consider it for its own collection? The owner was offering to sell it at the same price for which he had purchased it, and that figure seemed quite reasonable for a work of this period and quality. However, for budgetary reasons, the museum was really not in a position to acquire the painting. Yet it would have been almost criminal to allow the painting to leave Des Moines without making a serious attempt to place it.

And so I telephoned my friend Louise Noun.

In retrospect, I suppose I contacted her first because she is not only an ardent collector who has been trained as an art historian, but also because she is an avid feminist and the author of *Strong-Minded Women,* a book about the development of women's suffrage in Iowa (if one were to change the noun in the book's title from plural to singular, one would have an apt title for her autobiography). It seemed natural that Louise should have the first opportunity to acquire this imposing painting of women at work, depicted in a way that simultaneously highlighted their peasant simplicity and nobility. The fact that the artist herself was one of the pioneers of vanguard art of this century made it even more appropriate in my mind.

Once Louise saw the painting in the museum's storage rooms, she knew she had to have it, even though its price was many times what she had heretofore been accustomed to paying for works of art. Although Isabel Bishop, Suzanne Valadon, Marguerite Zorach, and one or two other women were already represented in her collection, Louise's decision to focus on women artists of the twentieth century began, she subsequently told me, with the purchase of the Gontcharova, and this emphasis has continued unabated ever since. Significant works by Rozanova, Münter, Höch, Kahlo, Hesse, and others found their way to her apartment. However, being female has not of itself guaranteed inclusion in the collection. For example, an oil painting by a well-known figure was returned to the dealer when Louise decided that the work did not hold its own among its peers. She preferred the directness and grittiness of Abastenia Eberle's sculptures of street urchins and poor immigrant women to the genteel refinement of Eberle's more famous friend, Anna Hyatt Huntington. As a result a sculpture by Eberle—which has since been donated to a museum—entered the collection, but none by Huntington (Noun's essay on Eberle remains the chief source of information about that under-appreciated artist). Similarly, after studying an etching by Cassatt for an unusually lengthy period of time, she decided ultimately that it was too saccharine for her taste. Her goal all along has been to concentrate not on famous names but on stimulating art.

It has been a source of considerable satisfaction for me to learn that Gontcharova and her many sisters in this exhibition will reside, through their respective works, in Iowa. And it has been a privilege to have played a small role in the growth of the collection, especially during the period from 1976 to 1984. Despite its tight focus and concentration, the collection is adventurous, inclusive but discerning, occasionally eccentric and unpredictable, and decidedly individualistic—not unlike Louise Noun herself. Long may she and her collection so remain.

James T. Demetrion, Director
Hirshhorn Museum and Sculpture Garden
Smithsonian Institution

In the catalogue that follows, dimensions are given in inches and centimeters in parentheses; height precedes width and depth. Titles are in italic type; alternate or descriptive titles are in parentheses. References in parentheses in the text refer to individual artists' bibliographies.

Catalogue

Ella Bergmann

German, 1896–1971

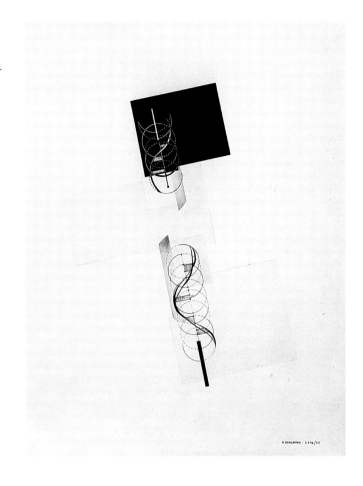

OB 193   circa 1924
Pencil and ink, 22 × 17 (55.9 × 43.2)
Provenance: Zabriskie Gallery, New York, 1984

Spiralisms-Picture   1927
Pencil, ink, and gouache on paper mounted on laminated
board, 24⅝ × 19⅜ (62.5 × 49.2)
Provenance: Zabriskie Gallery, New York, 1982

Ella Bergmann established the direction of her artistic career in 1923, when she and her future husband, Robert Michel, were expelled from the Weimar Art School. At that time, Bergmann and Michel were living in Vockenhausen and were showing with El Lissitzky and Kurt Schwitters at the Nassauischen Kunstverein in Wiesbaden. The significance of these artistic connections cannot be exaggerated. The group exhibited together again in 1925, and in 1927 Schwitters, Michel, and Bergmann traveled to Holland. In 1926, Bergmann placed a few works at the Mart Stam Haus in Stuttgart for an exhibition entitled "Werkebund." Her increasing stature as a proponent of European modernism induced the fabled Société Anonyme of the United States to include her works in a traveling exhibition entitled "Arts Council 1928."

Bergmann continued to exhibit until the early 1930s. When the cultural climate in Germany grew hostile to modernism, both she and Michel stopped all creative activity and turned to agriculture to survive. After the war, Bergmann lectured extensively on European modernism at the so-called American Houses, established in Germany by the Marshall Plan to promote cultural exchange, and she thereby influenced the relationship of an entire generation of German youth to modernity and culture.

The Bergmann works in the Noun Collection reflect the artist's fascination with blueprints, as well as her familiarity with El Lissitsky's design principles and his concept of the artist as a social engineer, creator of a new culture. Accordingly, the lines and shapes of these works are executed with the impeccable, mathematical precision of an architectural drawing. Yet it is clear that neither of these works is a literal plan for construction; Bergmann has applied her own aesthetic sense to what might be thought of as drafting exercises, using spirals and asymmetrically balanced movement to create works of great formal elegance. (The abbreviated "OB" in the title may stand for O[riginal] B[ild] or Original Picture.)

Bergmann's career was rekindled in the 1960s when she and Michel exhibited extensively in Europe and the United States. After her death in Vockenhausen in April 1971, her work was shown separately from that of Michel in 1974 in Germany and in 1984 in both Paris and New York.

S.V.

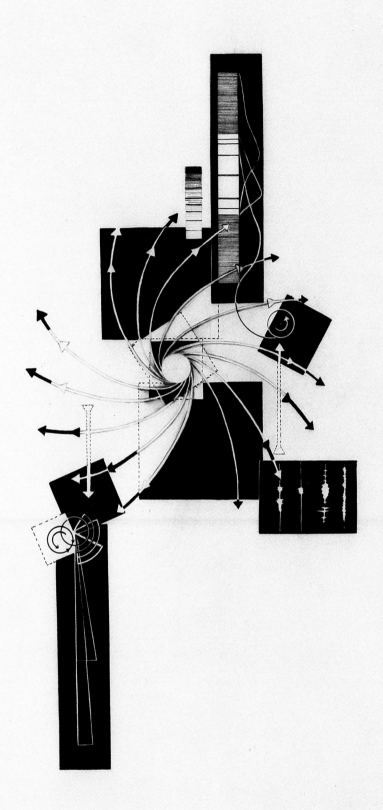

oB 193,
ELLA BERGMANN

Isabel Bishop
American, 1902–1988

During the 1940s and 1950s, Isabel Bishop's figurative style, which had developed under the enduring influence of her teacher and mentor, Kenneth Hayes Miller, was often espoused as a viable alternative to the emerging style of Abstract Expressionism. Although Bishop admired Pollock, Rothko, and other artists of that movement, and while she agreed that there was a certain rationale for a movement towards abstract art in the twentieth century, she asserted that for her the subject was preeminent.

> I believe this: that abstract art . . . can have content without subject. But the content is very generalized. It must be. It can be cheerful, it can be melancholy, it can be energetic or restful or exciting, but it couldn't deliver much of your relation to life, your experience, although aesthetically it is perfectly sound. Power in the art of painting exists at its height with the use of subject—content being within the subject and within the form. (Reich, 22)

In 1918, Bishop came to New York from her childhood home in Detroit and, at age sixteen, enrolled in the New York School of Applied Design for Women. Her plans to be an illustrator were discarded when she "heard of modern art" (Bishop in Reich, 19), and by 1920 she had begun classes at the Art Students League, where she studied with Max Weber, Guy Pène du Bois, and finally with Miller. In 1934 Bishop took a studio in Union Square, and for five decades she maintained an orderly schedule, commuting five days a week from her home in the Bronx to her studio, where she spent the day drawing and painting.

Throughout this period she worked exclusively with the human figure. Although her subjects are most often clothed and on the streets of New York, she regularly returned to the study of the female nude. Her fleshy nudes, caught in the act of dressing or undressing, and her delicate draftsmanship and subtle coloring betray her admiration for Fragonard, Rubens, Renoir, and Rembrandt. And yet she was fully aware of the need to move beyond tradition.

> The revolt against specific subject matter in painting and sculpture, in our period, was necessary—even overdue. And of all subjects . . . the nude should be questioned most severely. . . . Traditionally the nude was used to express formulations about life as larger-than-life or more-perfect-than-life; as Heroic or Ideal. But what shall provide the larger statement when these attitudes are rejected—as we do, in fact, reject them! My attempted solution is to try for mobility in the form. When mobility is introduced into a picture, the possibility is expressed that whatever is represented there can change its position, though all may be described as still. This communication . . . releases the content! Potential for change opens the door to so much. Were mobility achieved, the limitations of the specific subject could be both kept and transcended. (Lunde, 60–61)

Isabel Bishop was interviewed often, and it is clear that the need to depict mobility within the two-dimensional picture plane remained central to her artistic philosophy, regardless of the eccentricities of specific subject matter. She defined mobility as the potential for motion and set herself a lifelong project of depicting "the material and the immaterial as they intersect along the contours of the human body" (Munro, 146).

J.C.

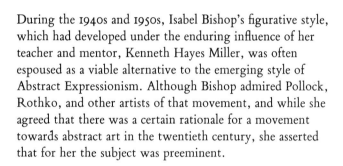

Isabel Bishop
American, 1902–1988

In the Subway (Women Walking in the Subway,
no. 2)   1963
Etching, 9¾ × 10⅜ (24.8 × 26.3)
Provenance: Gift of the artist

OPPOSITE, TOP:
Subway Station under Grand Central   1966
Etching, 8¾ × 15 (22.2 × 38.1)
Provenance: Midtown Gallery, New York, 1968

OPPOSITE, BOTTOM:
Women Walking, no. 1   1963
Oil and tempera on canvas, 36 × 40 (91.4 × 101.6)
Provenance: Midtown Gallery, New York, 1964

Isabel Bishop took as her subject the people of New York. In her early genre paintings they converse, eat, read, sit on bar stools or sleep on park benches, ride subways and buses, stoop to pick up cigar butts, or stop in mid-motion as they put on or remove their overcoats. In her later paintings the narrative content was diminished; Bishop's people stride by oblivious to one another, their figures dissolving into an orange-toned atmosphere broken by white dots and dashes. These dots and dashes produce a veil-like effect, enveloping the walkers and "weaving the figures and the surroundings together" (Bishop in Munro, 152), while at the same time they draw our attention to the surface of the painting and retain the very shallow picture plane Bishop sought. John Canaday has suggested that the technique gives the subjects "a kinetic character, some of the feeling of constant motion and change to which people in the city are subjected even when they are nominally at rest" (Reich, 35).

Bishop's walking pictures grew out of a series of sketches of the subway under Union Square. Fascinated with the architectural elements, the columns and exposed vaults, she spent a summer sketching the two-story interior, but when she added people to the compositions

> it seemed to turn into a prison. . . . The station was, after all, a place of movement, of going and coming. Gradually, I decided that the only way for me was to make the people ephemeral, transparent. Not fixed.

> So I had a model move along in a series of walking steps and I stopped her, as in the Muybridge photos. And so I drew a sort of frieze of gestures that I introduced into the scene as only the vaguest impressions. Later, I thought of using the frieze of figures themselves as the motifs for a painting. And that was my first walking picture. (Munro, 152)

Although Bishop's output of graphic works was exponentially higher than her production of paintings, she considered herself a painter, and all of her graphic works are studies for paintings. Her working method was slow and meticulous. She began with small, rough sketches, done in the streets, in Union Square, or while making her daily subway commute into the city from her residence in Riverdale in the Bronx. These preliminary sketches were reworked into more finished pen and ink or wash drawings.

Etchings and aquatints followed from there. Bishop studied printmaking with Stanley William Hayter and did her own printing, although she claimed no interest in experimentation with or exploitation of the possibilities of the intaglio process. Rather her interest lay in the development of spatial elements through the use of a single line. In order to anticipate changes in scale and the adjustments necessary when moving from graphics to larger panel paintings, Bishop next had the prints or drawings photographically enlarged. From there she began to paint, working several months on each panel. The entire process often took up to a year. "I struggle for months and months to make it look as momentary as it really is" (Bishop in Reich, 28).

In the Subway is one of the many drawings and prints done in preparation for the Noun Collection painting, *Women Walking, no. 1; Subway Station under Grand Central* found its culmination in a 1967 painting of the same title.

J.C.

6

Louise Bourgeois

American, born in 1911

Figure voile   circa 1949
Ink, 9¾ × 12¾ (24.8 × 32.4)
Provenance: Robert Miller Gallery, New York, 1986

Figure voile, like Louise Bourgeois' sculptural work, is deeply nostalgic. The seemingly abstract images in both her drawings and her three-dimensional work are direct expressions of personal experiences and memories. Childhood anxieties, as well as social and sexual conflicts of adult life, resurface and find resolution in her simplified, but richly suggestive, forms. (The title inscribed on this work — *figure-voile* — is enigmatic; the French words have no syntactical relationship to one another. The literal translation is "shape/sail" or "shape/veil.")

Bourgeois is perhaps best known for her powerful sculpture, although she has drawn continuously throughout her career. Her work has been characterized by her persistently experimental approach to forms, ideas, and materials. And like her sculpture, her drawings are explorations of her most deeply felt experiences. Bourgeois seeks a formal clarity that can transform and restate the complexity of the inner, psychological world without sacrificing its emotional truth or obliterating its contradictions.

As in all her work, the imagery in *Figure voile* is suggestive, ambiguous, and replete with multiple subjective associations. Bourgeois herself is the subject of her fertile imagination; all her work is an exploration of her self in its physical, as well as psychological, space. But this focus on self includes an examination of her relationship with others: her self is defined by its social context as well as its personal reality. The forms and textures of *Figure voile* allude to the undulating curves of the French landscape and to memories of her parents' tapestry workshop, which was located in the French countryside. The striated marks and the oblong, pendulous shapes recall the great skeins of wool that hung from beams in the workshop and the shuttles which her parents and their employees used in their trade. But, as is

true of all her work, the imagery in this drawing simultaneously represents aspects of her inner life as well as those of her personal history.

Direct references to objects and experiences of her childhood are fused with those of adulthood; anxieties from childhood merge with those of adulthood and share their forms in her art. That which recalls a skein of wool or a particular knoll in the French countryside also signifies human anatomy, sexual identity, and sexual anxiety. Speaking of landscape forms in her work, Bourgeois has said, "They are anthropomorphic and they are landscape also, since our body could be considered from a topographical point of view, as a land with mounds and valleys and caves and holes. It seems rather evident to me that our own body is a figuration that appears in Mother Earth" (Wye, 25).

Bourgeois' work presents the ambiguity of womanhood: vulnerability, claustrophobia, aggression, responsibility, pain, nurturance, protection, and eroticism, all of which are states of being through which women experience the world and through which women define their relationships with others in the world. These states of being are the recurrent subject of Bourgeois' work. She has said,

> Several years ago I called a sculpture *One and Others.* This might be the title of many since then: the relation of one person to his surrounding is a continuing preoccupation. It can be casual or close; simple or involved; subtle or blunt. It can be painful or pleasant. Most of all it can be real or imaginary. This is the soil from which all my work grows. The problems of realization — technical, and even formal and aesthetic — are secondary; they come afterwards and they can be solved. (Wye, 35)

J.S.

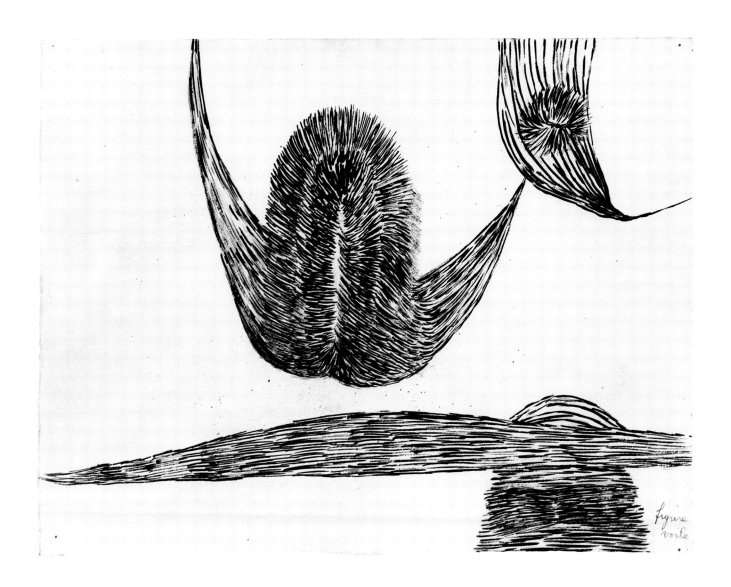

figure
voile

Leonora Carrington

English, born in 1917

Cannibal, no. 4
Pencil and ink, 9¼ × 13⅜ (23.5 × 34.0)
Provenance: Gallerie d'Arte, Mexico City, 1967

Among the brilliant and eccentric personalities of Surrealism, Leonora Carrington, artist and author, occupies a unique place. In fact, the story of her youth seems closer to gothic romance than biography. Carrington was born in Clayton Green, Lancashire, in 1917, the only daughter among the four children of wealthy textile manufacturer Harold Wilde Carrington and his Irish Catholic wife, Maureen Moorhead. Carrington's childhood years were spent at the family home, Crookhey Hall, near Lancaster, under the care of her Irish nanny and French governess. Expelled from two English convent schools because of her rebellious and unconventional behavior, Carrington was sent to boarding school in Florence and finishing school in Paris. Owing to her parents' position in society, she was presented at court (albeit reluctantly) in 1934, and in 1936 she left her family to study at the art academy of Amadée Ozenfant in London. There, at a dinner party, she met Max Ernst, whom she followed to Paris.

Ernst and Carrington lived together at Saint Martin d'Ardèche in southern France for two years until the onset of the war, when Ernst was interned as a prisoner. Carrington left Saint Martin d'Ardèche, suffered a mental collapse, and was institutionalized in a sanitorium in Santander, Spain. Released from the asylum in 1940, and destined by her parents for further hospitalization in South Africa, Carrington left Spain for Lisbon. Plans had been made to convey her via submarine to South Africa, but Carrington eluded her guardian during a supervised shopping trip, and took refuge in the Mexican consulate. The Mexican government protected her, and she was aided by Renato Leduc, a Mexican acquaintance whom she had first met through Picasso in Paris and whom she had recently reencountered in Madrid after her hospitalization.

Leduc and Carrington were married in Lisbon in 1941, moved to New York, and then settled in Mexico City, where they were amicably divorced a year later. In 1946 Carrington married her second husband, the Hungarian photographer Enrique Weisz, and she still resides in Mexico City today.

Carrington has been extremely productive as an artist and author, creating thousands of paintings, sketches, watercolors, and sculptures, and writing plays and stories. Two of her prose works from 1937, *The House of Fear* and *The Oval Lady,* were illustrated by Max Ernst. By 1944 Carrington's paintings were avidly collected by Edward James, the English patron of Surrealism. Among her more elaborate projects was the great mural, *El Mundo mágico de los Mayas,* which she created in 1962 for the National Museum of Anthropology in Mexico City. Of Carrington, Marina Warner has said:

> Widely read in alchemical writings, a regular pilgrim since 1971 to the lamas in exile from Tibet, analyzed by followers of Jung, and loyal to a fierce and personal brand of feminist idealism, Leonora Carrington never altogether sheds in her quest for wisdom a wonderful, saving mischievousness. (Warner, 20)

In addition to her important position as a Surrealist artist, Carrington has served as artist's muse. For Max Ernst, more than twenty-five years her senior, Carrington was a *femme-enfant* — an innocent child and sensual woman (Chadwick, 66–80). Aspects of Carrington's sexuality were often reflected in her early work, as was her preoccupation with animal imagery, a fact that Carrington attributed to her natural love of creatures and to the stories of Celtic folklore told to her as a child by her mother. For example, the horse, a symbol of independence, and the hyena, an emblem of sexuality and fertility, are frequent characters in her painting and prose. In Carrington's cosmos, animals are not mute creatures but anthropomorphized personalities. In the meticulous and detailed style of her writing and painting, separations do not exist between the human and animal kingdoms, for her creatures, like her imagination, know no bounds.

The two fearsome beings in the drawing *Cannibal, no. 4* seem unrelated to any of her larger designs. In their demonic dance, these primitive characters with their oversized heads and pliant bodies are worthy of Hieronymus Bosch, whom Carrington admires. Above and connected to the two cannibals, in finer, thinner lines, is the less detailed form of a fantastic flying animal. The free-flowing manner in which the principal group at the lower left is linked to the beast in the upper portion of the composition suggests the automatic drawings favored by the Surrealists.

H.F.

Sonia Delaunay-Terk
French, 1885–1979

Simultaneous Contrasts   1912–13
Watercolor, 10½ × 8⅛ (26.5 × 20.6)
Provenance: Artcurial, Paris; Barbara Mathes, New York, 1989

Although of Russian birth, Sonia Delaunay-Terk is considered one of the important figures of early twentieth-century French modernism. Born in 1885 of a Jewish family in a small village in the Ukraine, Delaunay-Terk was adopted at age five by a wealthy uncle, who raised her in the Francophilic culture of St. Petersburg. At a very early age she was exposed to many aspects of Western European culture; she became fluent in several languages, including French, and the Terk family had a sizable collection of paintings by members of the French Barbizon School. From 1903 to 1905 she studied art at the university in Karlsruhe, Germany, where her professor, Ludwig Schmidt-Reutter, continued her education in European modernism. From the start color was of foremost interest to Delaunay-Terk, and she was particularly attracted to Impressionism with its emphasis on color as its primary formal vehicle.

In 1905 Delaunay-Terk moved to Paris, around which she would center the rest of her life. Like many other young Russian artists, she studied at La Palette. In 1907 she became interested in the work of Paul Gauguin and Vincent van Gogh because of their use of bright, saturated colors as a means of expressing intense emotional states. That same year she met the painter Robert Delaunay, who shared her fascination with the formal potential of color. In 1909 she first became acquainted with many of the Cubist painters and writers, including Pablo Picasso, Georges Braque, and Maurice Vlaminck. This connection would be particularly important as the beginning of her discourse with the critic Guillaume Apollinaire and her friendship and collaborative relationship with the poet Blaise Cendrars. She married Delaunay in 1910, and in the same year she made a crib quilt for their newborn son; the quilt reportedly was declared a "cubist" piece by Delaunay-Terk's friends (Buck, 215) and,

in its stacking of geometric elements, it prefigures her signature style. It also marks the beginning of her application of artistic principles to objects outside the traditional limits of art, such as clothing, fabrics, and household objects.

It was in 1912, however, that Delaunay-Turk achieved her most significant breakthrough. While exploring different aspects of color theory, she and Delaunay began creating works based on a theory of color contrasts that Delaunay called "simultaneity." In a series that Delaunay-Terk entitled *Simultaneous Contrasts,* of which the Noun Collection watercolor is one, the basis of space and movement is color, not perspective or line or other geometric elements. Space is delineated and movement differentiated by the juxtaposition of different colors. In the Noun watercolor, for example, lines are implied by the edges of areas of color, as in the wedge of black against the blue, or the transparent gold merging with the magenta in the upper left corner.

This work is one of a series of watercolors painted by Delaunay-Terk for a lecture also called "Simultaneous Contrasts," presented in July 1913 in St. Petersburg. Between 1912 and the time of the October Revolution, Delaunay-Terk created several posters and book art projects; the most notable of the latter was her 1913 collaboration with Cendrars on the visual and literary poem *La Prose du Trans-sibérien et de la petite Jeanne de France.* However, her emphasis shifted to nontraditional arts at the end of 1917, when the revolution eliminated her private family income.

E.B.

CONTRASTES SIMULTANÉ

Sonia Delaunay-Terk
1912-13

à Stenebey amicalement
le petit souvenir Sonia Delaunay

Alexandra Alexandrovna Exter

Russian, 1882–1949

Composition   1916–17
Tempera on canvas, 19½ × 13½ (50.0 × 34.5)
Provenance: Annely Juda Fine Art, London, 1985

Alexandra Exter was an important member of the early
twentieth-century avant-garde. She was trained in painting
and the traditional fine arts. She is best known, however,
for her theatre design and especially for marionettes and
puppet theatre. Her paintings from the teens, however, laid
the groundwork for the aesthetic concerns which she maintained throughout her career.

The year 1916 marks the beginning of Exter's "Futuro-
Supremo-Constructivist" years. In contradiction to our
western European notions of the Russian avant-garde, terms
such as "Futurism," "Suprematism," and "Constructivism"
were not used strictly by the Russians, and in fact the
ideologies signified by these terms very often were
employed concurrently by many artists, including Exter.
Having maintained strong contact with different branches
of the Russian avant-garde, she assimilated many competing
ideas, especially those of Malevich's Suprematism, with its
spiritual mission, and Tatlin's materialist Constructivist
program.

In the teens the notion of the Russian *zwetopis,* or
"painting of color," was important to several Russian
artists, including Ivan Kliun, Olga Rozanova, and Exter
(Marcardé, 126). Color is used kinetically in *Composition.*
Although the use of the colored arcs reminds many scholars
of Robert Delaunay's Orphist works, which focus on light
itself, Exter was more interested in how elements such as
light and line, for example, would serve compositional
movement. She worked extensively with compositional
movement not only in painting but, from 1916 on, in
theatre, collaborating on several occasions with the theatre
producer Alexandr Tairov at the Chamber Theatre in Moscow.

E.B.

Natalia Sergeevna Gontcharova

Russian, 1881–1962

Fishers (Pond)   1909
Oil on canvas, 45⅞ × 40¼ (116.5 × 102.2)
Provenance: Mikhail Larionov, Paris; sold by Larionov at
Sotheby's, London, July 1, 1964, lot 121; Leonard Hutton
Galleries, New York; Maxwell Galleries, San Francisco;
Galerie de Seine, Paris; private collection, California, 1976

*The West has shown me one thing: everything it has is
from the East.*

So writes Natalia Gontcharova for the catalogue of her one-woman exhibition of 1913. Although *Fishers* was created in 1909, in many ways it typifies her belief throughout her career that, despite her debts to Western art movements, her artistic interests lay in the traditional life and work of Russia. Although she studied at the Moscow Institute of Painting, Sculpture, and Architecture, Gontcharova insisted that her real education did not begin until her trip to Paris in 1906. Here she became involved in the art community and exhibited in the Russian section of the 1906 Salon d'Automne. She knew the Fauvist and Cubist painters well. As her words suggest, she returned to Russia with very strong convictions about the potential of her work in the East.

Throughout her career, Gontcharova was deeply committed to a visual idiom that not only reflected but derived its energy from traditional Russian life. She was convinced that art cannot be taught in art academies or institutions, be they French or Russian; one must look to the common visual language of the people, to religious icons or signs of town merchants, for example. She also felt that the East was the source for all Western visual idioms.

Fishers particularly exemplifies Gontcharova's passion for the "primitive" elements in art, as opposed to rarefied academic standards. Like their Western contemporaries, Gontcharova and many other Russians sought to regain a basic, universally understood language in painting. She observed that while the Western artists she had met had to turn to other cultures, such as those of Madagascar, Tahiti, or pre-Columbian America (Bowlt, 58), the Russian artists had inherited a rich visual and cultural vocabulary that was still well preserved, especially in peasant life. The theme of this painting is the everyday labor of the peasants. The figures are dressed in traditional country work clothes; the woman wears a brightly patterned headscarf. These are the people whom Gontcharova knew all her life. She scorned artists like Gauguin for going outside of their own cultures and for ruining that which they found elsewhere (Bowlt, 58).

Gontcharova was certainly not the only Russian artist interested in peasant life; at this time genre painting was enjoying a new popularity in Russia. The *lubok*, or popular colored broadside, was an important source for her and many of her peers. In 1913 she and her partner, Larionov, organized an exhibition entitled "Icons and Lubki." In *Fishers* we see broad, flat areas of saturated color delimited by heavy outlines, not unlike the style of the mass-produced broadsides. Despite her admitted indebtedness to the Fauves, Gontcharova continually looked back to her own culture for sources and inspiration.

E.B.

Gertrude Greene

American, 1904–1956

Construction in Grey and Black   1939
Painted wood, 54 × 38¼ × 3 (137.2 × 97.1 × 7.6)
Provenance: The artist to Zabriskie Gallery, New York;
private collection, New York; Washburn Gallery, New
York, 1989

By the 1930s, when Gertrude Greene created the Noun
Collection relief, *Construction in Grey and Black,* the tenets of
the International Constructivist movement had been assimilated by the American avant-garde. American artists,
including Greene, helped to disseminate the principles of
Constructivism by producing and exhibiting their own
work that had been influenced by Constructivist aesthetics,
and by promoting both the art and the philosophy of European Constructivist artists. Greene, like many other American artists of the 1920s and 1930s, spent significant periods
of time in Paris, during which she became familiar with the
leading European abstract artists. Upon her return to the
United States, she produced and exhibited work that was
closely related to developments in European art, and that
placed her firmly in the American vanguard.

Greene visited Paris several times in the late 1920s. After a
six-month residency in 1931, she returned every two years
during the 1930s to renew her contacts with the avant-
garde, which by this date had established its international
headquarters in Paris. It was in 1931 that Greene became
acquainted with Constructivist principles through the work
of artists such as Naum Gabo, Antoine Pevsner, Piet
Mondrian, and El Lissitzky. Much of the theory espoused
by the Constructivists was socially oriented, if not utopian,
in its intent. Greene, however, adopted the forms and
mechanical aesthetics of Constructivism without adopting
its ideological and radical intentions.

During the 1930s, Greene became familiar with other
strands of modernist theory, and her work owes debts to
several of these influences. Laszlo Moholy-Nagy's formal
innovations, his experiments with new materials, and his
promotion of the machine aesthetic, in writings such as *The
New Vision,* were important influences on her work. And
while she was interested in the formal aspects of Surrealism,

she did not agree with its philosophy or its interest in illu-
sionism. Thus the limited palette and angular forms of *Construction in Grey and Black* reflect Constructivism's machine-
age aesthetics; its biomorphic forms recall the simplified
compositions of Jean Arp and Joan Miró; and the use of
wood and experimental construction techniques typifies the
twentieth-century exploration of media and composition
that began with Cubism. (Greene's interest in conservation
shows in her insistence on using wooden boards rather than
plywood in this work, and screws rather than glue to join
the pieces, fearing that glue might eventually degrade or
separate.)

Greene's interest in the European avant-garde did not pre-
vent her from participating in the contemporary American
art scene. As a founding member of the American Abstract
Artists, established in 1936 to promote avant-garde theories
and secure an American foothold for abstraction, Greene
joined a number of other artists who aligned themselves
with the international movement. During the 1930s
American art was dominated by Regionalism and social
realism; the A.A.A. presented an alternative direction for
art. It offered a forum for the exchange of ideas and
opportunities for exhibiting, which were not always readily
available to those who challenged the prevailing critics'
preferences in art. From the outset, and continuing for forty
years, the A.A.A. was an important force in the twentieth-
century American art world.

J.S.

Florence Henri

French-German, born in the United States, 1893–1982

Factory   circa 1924–25
Gouache, 11¼ × 9¾ (28.5 × 24.8)
Provenance: The artist; Martin and Ronchetti, Italy; Rachel
Adler Gallery, New York, 1986

Florence Henri was born in New York of French and German parentage. When she was only two years old her father moved to Europe for business reasons, and it was here that she would spend the rest of her life. A talented musician from an early age, she studied piano in England, Paris, Rome, and Berlin before abandoning music for the study of painting, which for Henri would include training at the Berlin Academy of Fine Arts, with Hans Hofmann in Munich and Alexander Archipenko in Berlin, at the Académie Moderne in Paris, and finally at the Bauhaus.

During a thirteen-year period between 1927 and 1940, Florence Henri created the constructionist photographs, portraits, and still lifes for which she is now most recognized. These works, begun under the tutelage of László Moholy-Nagy at the Bauhaus, undoubtedly drew sustenance from Henri's previous experiences at the Académie Moderne, where she studied in the atelier of Fernand Léger and briefly with Amédée Ozenfant from 1924 to 1926. During this period Léger made a brief foray into cinema, producing his revolutionary short Cubist film "Les Ballets mécaniques." In Léger's film, everyday objects, kitchen utensils and the like, are transformed into abstract composition by their multiplication and fragmentation in prismatic mirrors—a technique that Henri would later use to great success in her photographs.

An international artistic debate over the supremacy of abstract art versus non-objective art took shape at the closing of World War I. National and international artistic movements were defined and differentiated from one another by the position they took in this debate. In this Léger stood as a spokesman for abstraction. He espoused a "balance between the two poles of the real and the imaginary," stating that "to consider only one, either pure abstraction (objectless art) or imitation, is really too easy and evades the problem taken as a whole" (Fabre, 409). During her years at the Académie Moderne, Henri followed her mentor in both subject and technique. Works such as the Noun Collection gouache, entitled *Factory,* and a related oil of a similar industrial landscape, mirror Léger's utopian vision of a new union between modern man and modern technology. Léger's endorsement of industrialization is reflected in his impressions on leaving Chicago in 1931, when he writes of

a long and solemn procession of beautiful American factories at intervals all along the line for an hour. What a panorama! Huge chimneys with parallel strips of smoke streaming up into the sky, just like at a parade. . . . One dreams of a giant orchestra worthy of such a spectacle. The silhouettes of unidentifiables machines. Eighteen chimneys all in one stack, a huge organ. Majestic and final. (Broit, 274)

In *Factory,* Henri presents a rationalized and systematized composition of flat, overlapping planes and geometric forms, drawn from man-made objects, that is, buildings that were already geometric in contour. Her combination of geometric forms and the stylized human figure sets forth a world view that is at once modern and humanist. While Henri paintings of this period have sometimes been termed Purist—as described by Amédée Ozenfant and Charles-Edouard Jeanneret [Le Corbusier] in their 1918 manifesto, Purism is an art of rigidly disciplined abstraction, a return to Cubist simultaneity, a rejection of color, and an embracing of mechanical clarity as symbolic of the twentieth century as the age of the machine—her use of bright planes of color echoes Léger's theory of simultaneous contrast of form and color.

In 1925 Henri's works were included in "L'Art d'aujourd'hui," the first international exhibition of avant-garde art to be held in Paris after the war. "L'Art d'aujourd'hui" included Cubist, Purist, and Surrealist works by Léger, Willi Baumeister, Sonia and Robert Delaunay, Paul Klee, Ozenfant, and Hans Arp, as well as nonobjective pieces by Mikhail Larionov, Natalia Gontcharova, and Alexandra Exter. The dating of Henri's first nonobjective collages is a matter of debate, although she was without doubt working in that style by 1927 when she studied at the Bauhaus and took up photography, embracing the camera as the perfect instrument of the burgeoning industrial society. In the early thirties she was a member of the Cercle et Carré and Abstraction-Création, two vanguard artists' groups in which French Purism, Dutch De Stijl, Russian Constructivism, and Bauhaus abstraction briefly coalesced. Both groups dispersed with the outbreak of World War II, and Henri ceased her creative work. She all but gave up photography after the war, producing only a few photographic portraits, and returned to painting, creating during the last decade of her life a series of nonobjective collages reminiscent of those she had made in 1927 at the Bauhaus.

J.C.

F. Henri

Eva Hesse
American, 1936–1970

Magnet Boards 1967
Sculp-Metal on wood with magnets, 24 × 24 × 2
(61.0 × 61.0 × 5.0)
Provenance: Fischbach Gallery, New York; Mr. and Mrs. Henry Feiwel, New York; Sotheby's, New York, May 5, 1986, sale no. 5452, lot no. 40

Eva Hesse had a brief but very intense life and artistic career. She attended the Pratt Institute of Design, graduated from Cooper Union School of Art and Architecture, and in 1959 received her B.F.A. from Yale University. In 1964 she and her husband, artist Tom Doyle, went to Germany, where Hesse worked on her first major sculptures, previously having worked primarily as a painter. They returned to New York in the fall of 1965, and in the following spring Hesse participated in the Graham Gallery exhibition "Abstract Inflationists and Stuffed Expressionists." As the title suggests, the exhibition served as a reaction to the Minimalist painting and sculpture of artists such as Tony Smith, Kenneth Noland, and Frank Stella (Pincus-Witten, 35). The exhibition included the works of Frank Lincoln Viner, Philip Orenstein, Jean Linder, and Marc Morrel, and received generally negative reviews for its move away from slick, pared-down Minimalist forms. In September of that same year Hesse's works were featured in the exhibition "Eccentric Abstraction" at the Fischbach Gallery. It was curated by Lucy Lippard, who became Hesse's close friend, and featured Alice Adams, Louise Bourgeois, Gary Kuehn, Bruce Nauman, Don Potts, Keith Sonnier, and Viner. Like the spring show, the works reflected a "post-minimal sensibility" (Pincus-Witten, 37).

For Hesse and her peers, post-minimalism meant going beyond the pristine, industrialized forms of work by John McCracken and Stella. Rather, Hesse's work possesses a strong handmade quality. This emphasis is maintained even in her works from 1969 and 1970, when, because of several operations for a brain tumor, she gave precise instructions to her assistants in order to execute her ideas.

As Bill Barrette, who served as her assistant during the last year of her life, points out, *Magnet Boards* relates to several of her graph-paper drawings from 1967, with the emphasis on working within the structure of the grid (Barrette, 116). Originally she planned to use cords to connect the magnets from one box with those in another box. The previous year she had used this device in the series of wall pieces entitled *Metronomic Irregularity.* Although the Noun piece is the only one in which she uses magnets, Hesse frequently covered wood, steel washers, and other materials with Sculp-Metal, beginning in 1966.

Compositionally, *Magnet Boards* prefigures pieces such as the untitled work called "Washer Piece," and *Washer Table,* both from 1967, in its emphasis on individual units that have an assigned position within the whole. Barrette also notes, however, "the theme of randomness" (Barrette, 153) in much of Hesse's work from this time on. Despite an artist's attempt to make an arrangement appear random, "randomness ultimately requires aesthetic choices—which the idea of random dispersal was meant to circumvent" (Barrette, 16). In *Magnet Board,* which is made up of four boxes, Hesse addresses freedom of movement within prescribed bounds. In two of the four boxes, she laid out a grid into which the magnets fit. There is, however, no prescribed order, and without the cords, each magnet's position is independent, that is, each can be moved from box to box. Each magnet is meant to stay within a circumscribed territory (i.e., within a single unit of the grid) but is not bound to one location, a specific grid.

E.B.

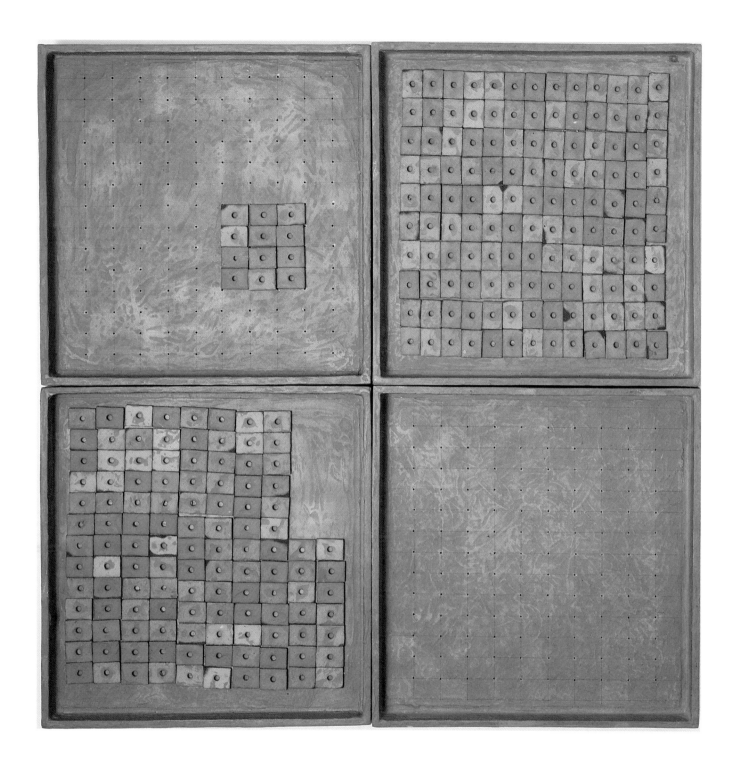

Hannah Höch

German, 1899–1978

The Path   1927
Oil on canvas, 37 × 25¼ (94.0 × 64.1)
Provenance: The artist to Fritz Schönthal; returned to artist
for safekeeping during World War II; from estate of artist
to Ruth Schönthal-Seckel (daughter of Fritz Schönthal);
Galerie Folker Skulima, Berlin, 1987

Perhaps Höch's most enigmatic painting and certainly one
of her most ambitious, *The Path* unites in a single composition a number of themes that the artist had already
elaborated in collages, watercolors, and paintings of the
early 1920s. Atop a high, curving wall divided into five
segments is a curious procession of human and animal figures who seem lit from within, so saturated are Höch's
glowing colors here. The entourage has come along the pre-
carious path from the back left, where an elderly man with
a walking stick is shown beside a large, blooming flower
and some stonelike objects resting on a dolly. Across the
first divide is a young nude couple, whose relationship is
symbolized by the salmon-colored, heart-shaped leaf against
which they are silhouetted. In front of them is a large child
with an oversized head, accompanying several sheep into a
nearby stand of evergreen trees. On the other side of the
trees, water birds, a giraffe, and an elephant enter a grave-
yard of a church from which a funeral procession has just
emerged. Pallbearers carrying an open coffin are accom-
panied by mourners, a priest, and a large woman dressed in
a long gray habitlike robe. Across the second divide are a
number of unidentifiable animals making their way toward
the third crevice in the wall. Beyond this is a segment with
mechanical objects and blocky architectural forms, as well as
two nude adults who are separated by a wilting plant. One,
a blue man with an oversized head and clawlike hands,
looks toward the other, a young woman with short hair
and an air of melancholy about her. At her feet are two
small babies and a large bird, who are approaching the
fourth divide. Finally, in the right foreground, is a large
blooming flower with a knifelike leaf that cuts across the
stomach of another nude woman, this one pregnant and
walking towards a cactus plant.

There is no firm evidence that this painting is autobio-
graphical in context, but there are certainly parallels between some of the imagery and Hannah Höch's life—
including the slender woman with the pageboy haircut who
bears a striking resemblance to the artist herself. If the story
begins with her childhood in the left background, the older
man walking beside a blooming flower may very well represent the artist's father, an avid gardener who imbued Höch
with a lifelong love of nature. Indeed, until her death Höch
worked almost as much on her garden in Heiligensee out-

side Berlin as she did on her art, using it as a source both of
relaxation and of inspiration for her work. In fact, it was
underneath the plants and flowers outside her back door
that Höch hid the "degenerate" art of her friends and colleagues during the Nazi regime, burying it in chests and
thereby saving much of it from certain destruction.

The pair beyond the man with the cane may represent
Höch and the artist Raoul Hausmann, with whom she had
her first serious relationship. By all accounts it was not an
easy partnership, one of the couple's many differences being
their views on children. Both wanted offspring badly, but
Hausmann was married throughout the entire relationship,
and Höch was unwilling to bear their child under those
circumstances (Maurer, 107–8). They finally separated in
1922, at which time Höch, partly in an effort to get over
Hausmann (Adriani, 72), hiked over the Alps from Munich
to Rome, where she found lodging in a cloister. Might not
the evergreens, the church, the funeral scene, and the
woman in a habit metaphorically represent this phase of
Höch's life, which ended, as it were, in the death of her
relationship with Hausmann?

It has been suggested by Ruth Schönthal-Seckel (daughter
of the original owner of the work) that the other prominent
male figure, the blue man with the large head, is Kurt
Matthies, whom Höch would later marry in 1938 after her
lesbian relationship with the Dutch poet Til Brugman
ended in 1935 (telephone conversation with Louise Noun,
March 1989). That marriage ended six years later in divorce,
with Höch laconically commenting, "I needed a child, he
needed a mother" (Ohff, 21). Indeed, even though Höch
was still involved with Brugman when she painted this
picture, thus rendering identification of the blue man as
Matthies problematic, the presence of the two yellow babies
and the pregnant woman at the very foot of the
composition (and the numerous images of babies in many of
her other collages and paintings of the period) indicate how
preoccupied Höch was in 1927 with the idea of children.

Finally, though, *The Path* resists definitive interpretation,
and this is indeed part of its magic. Like Höch's collages, it
is open-ended, piquing our curiosity with its enigmatic
forms and figures, and provoking speculation on their
meaning.

M.M.

Hannah Höch

German, 1899–1978

Two Children above the City   circa 1925
Collage on paper mounted on cardboard, 12⅜ × 8⅝
(31.4 × 21.9)
Provenance: La Boetie, New York, 1985

When in 1924 Germany finally managed to curb the run-away inflation that had torn the country apart since the end of World War I, the nation heaved a collective sigh of relief and turned its attention toward the many new diversions made possible by recent advances in modern technology. Innovations in audio and visual recordings, for example, brought cinema and radio to a broad public in the mid- to late-1920s, while advances in aviation turned thousands of Germans into flight devotees. But modern technology also affected German industry of the 1920s, and the changes in this arena were not so universally acclaimed. By 1925, when Hannah Höch made her collage *Two Children above the City,* rationalization—the term used to describe the variety of streamlining techniques adopted by German industry in the 1920s—had led to mass firings in many sectors.

This was no doubt among the reasons why Höch and her colleagues in the erstwhile Dada group (which, for all practical purposes, had disintegrated as a coherent movement by 1920) had serious reservations about technology. To be sure, on one level they saw the rational functioning of mechanized objects as a means of moving away from expressionist pathos toward greater clarity and neutrality in art. "Our whole purpose," Höch noted in a later interview, "was to integrate objects from the world of machines and industry into the world of art. Our typographical collages or montages set out to achieve this by imposing, on something which could only be produced by hand, the appearance of something that had been entirely composed by a machine" (Roditi, 26). But the Dadaists were well aware that the machine had also been an agent of the horrifying and irrevocable destruction of war, and they perceived it as a kind of vampire, which, if permitted, would suck the human spirit dry, transforming humankind into soulless objects as well.

Like many of her other collages, paintings, and watercolors of this period, Höch's photomontage *Two Children above the City* addresses the question of technology. Overlaid with a variety of mechanical parts is an aerial view of an industrial complex, which Höch no doubt took from a contemporary illustrated journal. Probably some of the technical objects, like the shiny nut and bolt at bottom center, came from advertising catalogues of the Knorr-Bremse firm, which Höch had already plundered for the machine imagery of her monumental collage of 1919, *Cut with a Kitchen Knife....* The precision of mass production is suggested throughout, from the evenly spaced rivets that hold together the segmented metal pipe at left, to the clean-cut lines of the nut and bolt at bottom center. But despite, or perhaps because of, their antiseptic purity, these technical objects are vaguely unsettling. The sinister buglike creature crawling atop the segmented pipe suggests what the floating "space station," just to the left and in front of the pointing hand, might ultimately evolve into, while the ridged, dark vertical object, rising out of the ground in front of the T-shaped building on the shore of the larger land mass, evokes images of artillery. In fact, this phallic shape hints that the industrial complex we see here in aerial view might very well be a military installation, as do the helmet at bottom center and the flagpole in the middle of the circular island. In this context the heavy-lidded gaze of the man in the bowler hat above seems threatening, and indeed, the woman at right regards him fearfully from over her shoulder.

Most of Höch's work resists definitive interpretation, and the 1925 collage *Two Children above the City* is no exception. But an oil painting done by Höch that same year, *Roma,* suggests that the key to this enigmatic work about modern technology may be found in the contemporary politics of Italy, which Höch had visited in 1920. By 1925 the country had become a totalitarian state under the Fascist Benito Mussolini, who then—having already used Italian troops to invade the Greek island of Corfu in 1923—was threatening the world with an aggressive imperialist foreign policy.

In *Roma* Höch put Mussolini at the center of a composition framed by scenes of St. Peter's. Wearing a bathing suit and a bowler hat, he stands beside Asta Nielsen, a Danish theatre and film actress whom Höch greatly admired and who here orders Mussolini off the world stage with a commanding gesture. The male and female faces in *Two Children above the City* also bear the features of Mussolini and Nielsen, but now the actress's rejection of the dictator is signified by a single hand pointing upward to two oversized children. Like Nielsen herself, whose fame was based on her portrayal of masculine roles such as Hamlet, the children in the Noun collage are androgynous, their male trousers at odds with their smiling female faces. They sit on a tightrope, swinging their legs playfully and, apparently, laughing at the military complex below them. Like the small boy in *Promenade . . . ,* they are the antidote for a sick European society that would use modern technology to subjugate other peoples, signified in Höch's collage, no doubt, by the poignant head of a small and very vulnerable black child, floating to the left of the pointing hand.

                                                                M.M.

Hannah Höch
German, 1899–1978

Tailor's Flower   1920
Collage, 20¼ × 17¼ (51.4 × 43.8) (with frame)
Provenance: Galerie Nierendorf, Berlin; Marlborough
Gallery, London; A. E. Bergman, Chicago; Galerie Folker
Skulima, Berlin; La Boetie, New York, 1981

Between 1916 and 1926 Hannah Höch was employed at the
Ullstein Verlag, one of Germany's largest publishing
houses, which produced books as well as popular journals.
Höch worked in the handicrafts department, making lay-
outs for texts and designs for vignettes, lettering, and illustrations. These were then used both in individual brochures
on sewing, needlepoint, embroidery, knitting, and crocheting, and in the bimonthly two-page spread on women's
crafts in *Die Dame,* Ullstein's equivalent of today's *Cosmo-
politan* or *Vogue. Tailor's Flower* is one of numerous Höch
collages of the early Weimar period that draw on such
designs. Here she has juxtaposed the paper patterns used in
sewing, with their flowing boldface lines that mark the
scissor's cut and their broken lines that trace the seamline,
against the gridlike background of a reproduction of needlepoint mesh. She then surrounded the image with other
objects used in sewing, first with a line of alternating snaps
and hooks and eyes that are attached to the inner lip of the
work's wooden frame, and then with one half of a zipper
that runs around the middle of the frame in an unbroken
line. The dancelike yet structured rhythm set up by these
various man-made elements is countered by an image of one
lone organic form, a delicate orange flower at the very
center of the collage.

On one level, of course, *Tailor's Flower* is about traditional
women's handiwork. For centuries, sewing, embroidery,
crocheting, needlepoint, and knitting had been the leisure
activities of upper- and middle-class women, while the less
affluent used their skills at such crafts as a means of income
that did not require them to leave their children alone at
home. Höch no doubt respected such specifically female
skills and the context in which they were put to use, for—
her Dada leanings notwithstanding—she was in many ways
very traditional, believing firmly, for example, in the value
of institutions like marriage and family. Thus, though some
of her Dada colleagues might very well have poked fun at
these accoutrements of women's handicraft, Höch treated
them with the utmost respect.

But *Tailor's Flower* is also about a different, far less time-
honored role of women in German society. Höch was
inspired to use the snaps, hooks and eyes, zippers, and paper
patterns—the signs, as it were, of traditional women's

work—by her job at Ullstein, which was fairly *un*traditional. Indeed, although it was not uncommon for women
in prewar Germany to work outside the home, it was the
outbreak of World War I and the massive deployment of
German men that brought women into the work force en
masse. The end of the war and demobilization saw the
return of many of these women to hearth and home, but
vast numbers either remained at their jobs, like Hannah
Höch, or took new ones outside the confines of the family.
To be sure, this was but an illusory emancipation for many,
who now shouldered a double burden. Away from the
home for much of the day, they nevertheless still remained
the primary caretakers of both the house and the family—a
fact that explains in part the extraordinary support that
women voters later gave the National Socialists, whose
platform included the return of women to "Kinder, Küche,
Kirche" ("children, kitchen, and church"). But others in
the Weimar Republic, especially single or childless women,
clearly enjoyed the benefits of their new occupational status.

Höch refers to none of this directly in *Tailor's Flower,* but
merely by using materials that she worked with every day
at her job at Ullstein, she alludes to the new professional
roles that women were beginning to fill in Weimar Germany. Höch also refers in *Tailor's Flower,* (*Schneiderblume*),
to her other profession, which for a woman was still
unusual: that of an artist. For although the German term
Schneider means "tailor" or "dressmaker," the word derives
from the verb *schneiden,* "to cut," with a knife, scissors, or
any other sharp implement. *Schneiderblume* thus refers both
to tailor's work and to the work of the collagist or photo-
montagist—the "cutter" par excellence, whose primary
technique is to snip images from newspapers, journals,
pamphlets, and photographs and reconstitute them in new
forms.

Tailor's Flower, then, is about both traditional and
untraditional women's activities, which, Höch seems to say,
are not mutually exclusive. To the contrary, the artist's
obvious respect for the materials of conventional women's
handicrafts together with her *un*conventional use of these
materials suggests that, for Höch, the ideal "New Woman"
of Weimar was one who altered but did not necessarily
reject out of hand more traditional female roles.

M.M.

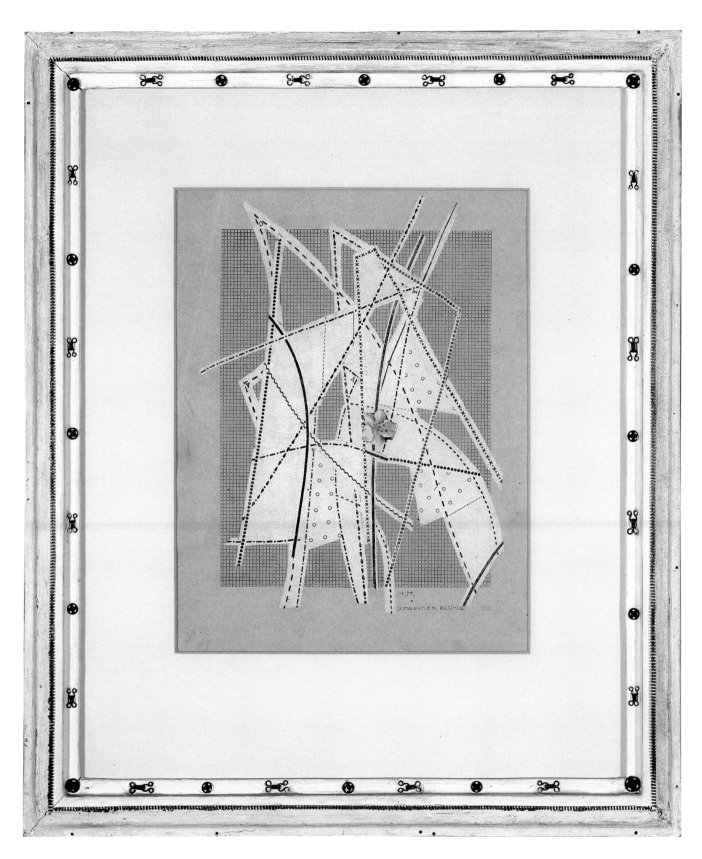

Hannah Höch

German, 1899–1978

Promenade . . . instructive, liberating, illuminating   1919
Collage, 12⅝ × 10⅞ (32.0 × 27.6) (with frame)
Provenance: Galerie Nierendorf, Berlin; La Boetie, New
York, and Galerie Folker Skulima, Berlin, 1984

For those like Hannah Höch on the left of the political
spectrum, disillusionment with the German Revolution and
the Weimar Republic came all too soon. The initial flush of
revolutionary utopianism in the cultural arena paled rapidly
in the face of political, social, and economic chaos, and the
ecstatic, transcendental note of Höch's 1919 watercolor
Circling Forms and of much other contemporaneous German
art was quickly toned down. Her 1920 photocollage
Promenade . . . illustrates the new sobriety that permeated
German art in the second decade of the twentieth century.

Photocollage—or photomontage, as it is alternately
known—recombines disparate images from printed periodi-
cals, newspapers, posters, and leaflets in surprising and often
disturbing ways. Höch, undoubtedly the most skillful of
her colleagues who worked with this new medium, came
well prepared to the enterprise. As a child she had not only
experimented with collage, making pictures out of shapes
cut from colored paper, she had also compiled books of
images snipped from magazines. Years later in Berlin she
returned to the medium of collage, creating abstract
pictures from bits of torn paper. But the real inspiration for
photomontages like *Promenade . . .* was her encounter with a
technique used by official photographers of the Prussian
army. By inserting portrait photographs of soldiers' faces
into generic oleolithographed mounts that represented
uniformed men in front of barracks or landscape scenes, the
photographers created personalized pictures that the soldiers
could send home or keep as mementos. These so impressed
Höch and her companion Raoul Hausmann that they began
to make their own montages.

Promenade . . . is a superb example of Höch's early
Weimar photomontages. With its elegant composition and
softly modulated tones keyed to harmonize with the colors
of its surrounding frame, it is eloquent testimony to the
continued importance of aesthetic considerations for at least
some members of the Dada group. Indeed, Höch, like her
friend and colleague Kurt Schwitters, wanted all her work
to be able to be experienced purely on an artistic plane, and
she was known among her colleagues for her speeches on
the value of art in postwar Weimar society. Still, the
aesthetic strength of *Promenade . . .* does not undercut its
social message, which Höch typically delivers with tongue-
in-cheek irony. Here, a man in gray topcoat and bowler hat
is out for a walk. Self-absorbed and self-satisfied, he seems

to be a most punctilious man, whose straight-laced attitudes
are summed up in the inscription above his head that pro-
claims the "Förderung des mittelstandlichen," or the
"Advancement of middle-class (values)."

It was precisely these values that Höch and the Dadaists
opposed. Indeed, though the specific cast of their politics
differed considerably, the Dadaists all despised what they
believed was the bourgeois complacency of the Social
Democrats (who, with all the other middle-class parties,
had voted for the war credits in 1914, and who were now
brutally murdering their own countrymen), and they all
celebrated Communism in one form or another. "As young
people who never believed in the justice of the German
cause in the war," Höch later noted of the Dadaists' early
attraction to Communist ideals, "we were still idealistic
enough to found our hopes only on those doctrines, which
seemed to be entirely new, in no way responsible for the
predicament in which we found ourselves, and to promise
us with some sincerity a better future, with a more
equitable distribution of wealth, of power, and of leisure"
(Roditi, 26). Not surprisingly, Höch and her colleagues all
idealized the worker, the proletarian, who seemed to them
spiritually untainted and—like a child—innocent, a model
for a middle-class society gone sour.

It is thus not mere coincidence that the buttoned-up
burgher of *Promenade . . .* is sandwiched, as it were, between
Russian letters peeking out from the blue sky at the top
left—an oblique but unmistakable reference to the successful
proletariat revolution in Russia—and a child at the bottom
right. Disproportionately larger than the man behind him,
he refuses to conform. He has removed his hat to reveal a
mass of unkempt red hair, and he stands with his legs apart
and his arms outstretched, the very image of spontaneous
joie de vivre next to his proper, self-contained counterpart,
whom he regards quizzically. Even the boy's sweater seems
to have a mind of its own, its rust tones refusing to remain
within their given contours and bleeding into the orange
background. Surely the other rooftop inscription—"Lehr-
reich, befreind und klärend" ("instructive, liberating,
illuminating")—refers to him. Like the Russian Revolution,
his playful innocence and childish refusal to conform to the
norm can be a model, Höch seems to tell us, for us all.

M.M.

Hannah Höch

German, 1899–1978

Circling Forms 1919
Watercolor, 18⅝ × 15⅞ (47.3 × 40.3) (sight)
Provenance: The artist to a private European collection;
Carus Gallery, New York, 1978

By her own account, Hannah Höch began to experiment with abstraction in 1915 (Roditi, 24) a full four years before she made the lyrical watercolor *Circling Forms.* At that time Höch was in Berlin, where she was exposed to a variety of influences that undoubtedly piqued her interest in nonrepresentational imagery. Not only was she regularly attending the exhibitions at Herwarth Walden's Sturm Gallery, since its opening in 1912 probably the most important venue in Berlin of abstract art, she was studying with Emil Orlik in his graphic course at the State School of the Museum of Decorative Arts. Here, her training was primarily geared toward using the two-dimensional elements of line, shape, color, and form in designs for three-dimensional utilitarian objects. The sort of abstract visual thinking that such an enterprise entailed was also necessary at the School of Decorative Arts in Berlin Charlottenburg, where Höch had begun her training in 1912 in the glassmaking class of Harold Bengen. There she must have grappled with the problems of a medium that is, to some degree, illusionistically handicapped by its dependence on a formal vocabulary of bold, simple shapes and flat, unmodulated color.

Höch made *Circling Forms* years after her training with Bengen, but it is not difficult to see in it the vestiges of his influence. In fact, the abstract *Circling Forms* might very well serve as a design for a stained glass window. Not only do its simple geometric shapes and skeletal framework recall the effect of cut glass set within a leaded armature, its softly glowing tones evoke the luminosity of backlit colored glass. Indeed, the compositional transition from the predominantly dark, rectilinear shapes below, into the light, curvilinear "circling forms" above, reproduces the feeling of spiritual transcendence that typifies an experience of viewing brightly illuminated stained glass from within a dark cathedral.

Notably, transcendence was a common theme in the work of German artists of this time. The utopian mood arose in the last year of World War I, following the Bolshevik Revolution in Russia in November 1917 and the consequent peace treaty between the Soviet government and the Central Powers in April 1918. With the ideas of socialism and peace thus inextricably intertwined in German consciousness, the armistice that concluded the war in the fall of 1918 and the November Revolution in Germany inspired the fervent hope in many Germans on the left of the political spectrum that their country was now on the upswing. To be sure, there were numerous pessimists, who increased in number as the collusion of the Weimar government with the military became apparent in the course of 1919. But at least initially many German artists believed that the new socialist government could yoke the communal forces that had once supported military adventurism and home-front sacrifice to social transformation and postwar rebuilding. Often using a cubo-expressionist vocabulary of geometric shapes, like those of *Circling Forms,* these artists created a body of work that expressed their utopian aspirations. Höch was one of those gripped by the utopian spirit of the moment. She joined the November Group, one of the numerous artists' organizations that sprang up in the early days of the Weimar Republic. Formed under mainly Expressionist leadership, the group's program was based in part on the notion that art had the power to effect spiritual renewal, and it staked a claim to participate in this renewal by demanding a voice in shaping official policy on the visual arts, specifically with regard to town planning, art school and museum reform, and provision of exhibition space. Höch later recanted her support of the organization when she signed the "Open Letter of the November Group Opposition," a document published in the periodical *Der Gegner* in 1920–21 that criticized the Novembrists' high-flown rhetoric and accused them of bourgeois complacency leading to depolitization. But together with works like *Circling Forms,* with their ecstatic coloration and their transcendent imagery, her early membership in the November Group indicates the great hopes that Höch, along with many other left/liberal Germans who had just suffered through the trauma of World War I, initially held out for the Weimar Republic.

M.M.

Hannah Höch

German, 1899–1978

Chinese Girl with Fan　　1926
Collage, 11 × 8 (27.9 × 20.3)
Provenance: Mayor Gallery, London; La Boetie, New York,
1989

This collage—which includes a photograph of a smiling young Chinese girl silhouetted against rectilinear fields of yellow, orange, and gray and surrounded by photographed fragments of fans—is unusual in Hannah Höch's oeuvre in terms of both technique and subject. Höch usually composed her collages by cutting images from a variety of sources with scissors or a razor, and then reassembling these disparate materials into a single, unified montage. As she herself said, with their precise, clean-cut edges, and the seamless way in which their components fit together, such works frequently give "the appearances of something that had been entirely composed by a machine" (Roditi, 26). In fact, the efficacy of such montages often depends in part on tricking the viewer into reading them not so much as handmade collages, but as photographic records of a world distorted in scale and form. By contrast, the torn (*not* cut) edges of the photograph of the child and of the piece of printed paper in *Chinese Girl with Fan* pointedly draw attention to the handmade process by which the work was put together, just as the bumpy, textural surface of the paper in the reproductions of the fans frankly declares its handmade origins. Indeed, this work seems to celebrate what is often disguised in Höch montages—that is, their origins in paper. It can hardly be coincidental that Höch chose a Chinese girl as the subject of this homage to the medium she most frequently used. For although the image of an Oriental child is uncommon in Höch's work (which often represents children, but almost never non-Western children), what could be more appropriate in a collage that commemorates the uses of paper, which had been invented in China centuries before?

As with most works by Höch, though, there is probably another level of meaning to *Chinese Girl with Fan*. In 1926 Höch traveled to Holland at the invitation of Kurt Schwitters. There she met the Dutch poet Til Brugman, with whom she began a lesbian relationship that lasted nine years. Brugman was friendly with the artists of the De Stijl group, especially with Mondrian, and through her Höch—who already knew a number of the De Stijl artists from her previous association with Schwitters, Hans Arp, Sophie Taeuber-Arp, and Theo and Nellie van Doesburg—was drawn into the Constructivist circle. Not surprisingly, the works she made in Holland, where she remained until 1929, often show this group's stylistic and thematic influence. In *Chinese Girl with Fan* the flat, rectilinear fields of color behind the child and the fan fragments recall paintings by Mondrian or van Doesburg, while the Chinese girl bears witness to the De Stijl artists' fascination with theosophy and its roots in Oriental philosophy and religions. Indeed, Höch even calls attention to the faith of the Chinese girl by dotting her forehead with a bit of photographed lace, which functions here as an *urna,* the traditional Buddhist symbol of spiritual insight.

Yet it is to Höch's great credit as an artist that she did not lose sight of herself while integrating elements of De Stijl into her work. To the contrary, she was very much aware of the inherent differences in her own essentially intuitive approach to art making and the De Stijl artists' more deliberate manner of working. "I could understand Mondrian's art," she later remarked, "but I never felt any need for as rational a style. I need more freedom and, though capable of appreciating a style that is less free than my own, have always preferred to allow myself a maximum of freedom" (Roditi, 29). Ultimately, the torn, ragged edges of the paper fragments in *Chinese Girl with Fan,* with their frank avowal of the work's handmade origins, are symbols of this artistic freedom.

M.M.

Gwen John
Welsh, 1876–1939

Chloë Boughton-Leigh   circa 1910
Pencil, 8½ × 5¾ (21.6 × 14.6)
Provenance: Artist's estate, no. EJ-885; Davis and Langdale
Co., New York, 1984

Until some fifteen years ago, the career and reputation of
Gwendolyn Mary John was overshadowed by that of her
more famous brother, the bohemian artist Augustus John
(1878–1961). The two middle siblings of four children born
to a strict Welsh Protestant lawyer, Edwin John, and his
wife, Augusta (née Smith), Gwen and Augustus John
shared their youthful penchant for art, and as children they
sketched incessantly. In 1894 Augustus moved to London to
enter the Slade School, the art academy renowned for its
emphasis on drawing. He was joined there a year later by
Gwen. Both siblings were gifted draftsmen and both won
prizes at the Slade School for drawing and composition,
but, to a great extent, Gwen's personal life and career were
inextricably bound to the personality of her dominant and
domineering brother. In 1898 she traveled to Paris with two
of her school friends, one of whom, Ida Nettleship, married
Augustus in 1901. Yet another friend, Dorothy (Dorelia)
McNeill, was so magnetized by Augustus that she became
his mistress, and eventually they married. Perhaps to escape
the powerful influence of her brother, Gwen John remained
permanently in France after 1903, where she lived until her
death in 1939.

Throughout her career the subject of John's work was
relatively consistent: she painted and drew the circumscribed sphere of her own domestic existence—her friends,
acquaintances, pets, and her immediate surroundings. With
circumspection and deliberation she repeatedly returned to
these themes in small studies of women and children. Typical of the relationship between her sketches and paintings,
and representative of her talent as a draftsman, is this sketch
of Chloë Boughton-Leigh.

Ellen Theodosia Boughton-Leigh (1868–1947), known to
her friends as Chloë, was the daughter of Edward
Boughton-Leigh of Brownsover House, near Rugby,
Warwickshire, and the older sister of Maude (Grilda)
Boughton-Leigh. Both sisters had studied at the Slade and
traveled periodically to Paris, where Gwen John probably
met them around 1907 (Langdale, 1987, 115–16). John's first
oil portrait of Chloë, now in the Tate Gallery, dates from
this time. Cecily Langdale has pointed out that the relationship between the sisters and John was initially rather cool
and formal, and judging from extant correspondence, it
appears that John was initially resentful of their pressuring

her to complete a second portrait of Chloë (Langdale, 1987,
140). In time, as Chloë Boughton-Leigh sat for John and
John modeled for Grilda, their relationship became more
cordial and strengthened. Chloë Boughton-Leigh maintained a lifelong correspondence with John, which, in addition to messages from Grilda on artistic matters, concerned
issues such as John's personal health, the care of her cats,
and books. Often included in the correspondence were
presents of food and clothing for John in Paris.

Gwen John sometimes drew sketches before carrying out
her paintings, although the drawings rarely served directly
as preparatory studies for her oils. The Noun Collection
drawing of Chloë Boughton-Leigh seems closely connected
to John's second oil portrait of her, which is now in the
Leeds City Art Gallery. It is also similar to other drawings
of this period that have been linked to the Leeds oil. Cecily
Langdale has published three sketches of Chloë in pencil and
wash, dated to 1910, which she has connected to the Leeds
portrait: *Bust of a Woman* (Albright-Knox Art Gallery);
Portrait of Chloë Boughton-Leigh (collection of Carter
Burden); and a study for *Les Suppliantes* (private collection).
To these works can be added two other pencil and wash
drawings in private collections (Taubman, 32–33, 115–16).

While the drawing in the Noun Collection is similar to
all of these pencil and wash drawings in size, in its bust-
length format, and in the sitter's age, it seems even more
closely related to the Leeds portrait than some of the other
studies for several reasons. First, as in the oil, Chloë
Boughton-Leigh is turned in three-quarter profile. Second,
her hair is arranged in a casual style, with the back upswept
and fastened at the top of her head in a chignon or bun.
Third, the pleats or shirring on the front of the dress in the
painting are suggested in the treatment of sketchy parallel
lines in the drawing. Finally, the sitter's sloping, rounded
shoulders, slightly stooped posture, and distracted gaze are
common to both the drawing and the painting.

Gwen John's talents as a draftsman are readily apparent in
this sketch. With great economy she suggests the introspec-
tive mien of Chloë Boughton-Leigh. In the few unruly
wisps of hair and a body language of boredom and dejec-
tion, John evokes the complex character of the person
beneath the surface (Bass, 148).

H.F.

Gwen John

Welsh, 1876–1939

House with Lamp Post, Evening   late 1920s(?)
Gouache, 12¼ × 9¼ (31.1 × 23.5)
Provenance: Artist's family; Anthony d'Offay, Ltd.,
London, 1985

Gwen John's "interior life"—as a recent exhibition of her work was called—consisted of an intense scrutiny of the people and places she knew intimately (Langdale, 1985). In 1903 John settled on the Continent. By 1904 she had set up her own small studio in Paris, and she began to model for other artists to earn money. At around this time, in the atelier of a fellow artist, John met Auguste Rodin, who was to have a profound impact on her life. For over a decade she maintained an intermittent and sometimes passionate liaison with him, serving also as a model for this legendary sculptor.

In January 1911, while keeping her small Parisian studio on the rue de l'Ouest, John moved to 29 rue Terre Neuve in Meudon, southwest of Paris, to be near Rodin, who lived in the town. The rooms which John rented there were part of a large house on a road rising to the Bois de Meudon observatory terrace. On November 21, 1910, the artist enthusiastically wrote to a friend from the Slade School, Ursula Tyrwhitt, describing the arrangement:

> Now I am going to tell you my little joy—I have taken a flat in Meudon . . . I am only going to possess it in January. . . . It costs only forty-five francs every three months . . . it is the top story of an old house quite near the forest . . . there are three rooms and a little kitchen and heaps of cupboards and a *grenier* [attic]. (Langdale, 1987, 49)

The building represented in the gouache *House with Lamppost, Evening* resembles John's lodgings on the rue Terre Neuve. Like the Meudon house, this building, with its pitched roof and large windows, is set on a pronounced incline amid luxuriant foliage. John flattened the image in the gouache by choosing a low viewpoint, filling the space with the house and trees, and placing the building and

foliage relatively high on the picture plane. From 1911 to the early 1920s John painted a number of representations of the street and area. The general character of the terrain depicted in the Noun drawing, with its steep street and verdant hedge, and the artist's gray and green palette, strongly suggest a relationship to other works representing the vicinity around John's home in Meudon.

H.F.

Frida Kahlo
(Magdalena Carmen Frida Kahlo y Calderón)
Mexican, 1907–1954

Self-portrait with Unbound Hair   1947
Oil on Masonite, 23⅝ × 17⅜ (60.0 × 44.1)
Provenance: Licio Lagos, Mexico City; Mary-Anne Martin
Fine Art, New York, 1983

Frida Kahlo created a personal, original art in which she portrayed herself, the pain, and the love that were the most important facts of her existence. At the age of eighteen she was seriously injured in a traffic accident. She lived in pain for the rest of her life; underwent dozens of operations, an amputation, abortions; was unable to bear a deeply desired child; attempted many suicides; and was desperately dependent on painkilling drugs. Nevertheless, she lived a very full life, with a cheerfulness that defied her suffering. She knew "everybody," was active as a committed Communist, and had a long, stormy marriage with Diego Rivera. Kahlo was a highly productive artist and was well recognized. Originally self-taught, her style was a modernist fusion of Mexican folk art and Surrealism.

Kahlo worked to create a legend around her own life. She often lied about her age, claiming to be a child of the Mexican Revolution of 1910. In *Self-portrait with Unbound Hair* she gives her age as thirty-seven, but she had in fact already turned forty. Kahlo depicts herself against a rough wall of the house in which she was born. Located in the Mexico City suburb of Coyoacán, it was built by her parents in 1904 and is today the Museo Frida Kahlo. In 1947, the year of this painting, Kahlo was recuperating from spinal fusion surgery, which she had had in New York in June 1946. She had spent the next eight months bedridden, in a steel corset; at the time she painted this work she had just been liberated from this device. Although many of Kahlo's self-portraits show her as a wounded being, even split open, this painting has no overt references to her ordeal.

Here Kahlo is dressed in a short-sleeved red dress topped by a yellow-gold vest with a diamond appliqué pattern. From the 1920s on, Kahlo and other Mexican intellectuals adopted and promoted ethnic Mexican style. Native clothing and other goods were all used in preference to bourgeois European items. Aside from taste, this had political significance in line with the revolution and with the Communist ideal of the solidarity of the people. For Kahlo it also had much to do with the image she wanted to create for Rivera, whose own art was based on the fusion of heroic images of indigenous Mexican peoples, modern art, and politics.

For Frida the elements of her dress were a kind of palette from which she selected each day the image of herself that she wished to present to the world. People who watched the ritual of her dressing recall the time and care she took, her perfectionism and precision. (Herrera, 110)

In this work Kahlo shows herself with loose hair, although in most of her self-portraits her hair is braided, crowned with Mexican lace, headdresses, or flowers, or interlaced with ribbons. The paintings which do show her with loose hair mostly date from the 1940s. Most of these paintings deal with her surgery, or have an intimate quality that refers to a nonpublic Frida. Photographs show that Kahlo generally wore her hair loose when she was in bed, which she was in much of 1946–47. Although the portrait is "a reflection," it really combines two different reflections. The eyes and mouth are seen frontally, while the nose is turned a few degrees to her right. The work combines two opposing traditions of representing the human countenance: the icon and the informal portrait of a human being. Kahlo previously painted herself in iconic form and she was certainly not the first artist to do so. The most famous example of this is Albrecht Dürer's *Self-portrait* of 1500, in which he painted himself as a blessing Christ. The artist's position and the great mass of long hair, as well as the artist's self-conception, make one wonder if Kahlo knew this famous Dürer self-portrait.

In contrast, informality, such as the off-center part in her hair, offsets the iconic quality of the Noun Collection painting. The hair cascading over her left shoulder is nicely balanced by the donkey's tail, a succulent plant, growing out of the obsidian-encrusted wall. Her acceptance and depiction of her flawed beauty makes this a portrait of a human being, not an abstraction. Kahlo's achievement was to make her physical and emotional suffering the subject of her art, not merely the motivation of it, and to transform it into something rare and wonderful. Her unrelenting focus on herself and the trials she endured give her work an extraordinary inpact. *Self-portrait with Unbound Hair,* without being bizarre or painful, incorporates much of what is essential about Frida Kahlo.

A.W.

Aquí me pinté yo, Frida Kahlo, con la imágen del espejo. Tengo 37 años, y es el mes de Julio de mil novecientos cuarenta y siete. En Coyoacán, México, lugar donde nací.

Erika Giovanna Klien

Austrian, 1900–1957

Tower Caving In/Ober St. Viet   1922
Black crayon, 11⅝ × 6⅞ (29.5 × 17.5)
Provenance: Galerie Pabst, Munich; Rachel Adler Gallery,
New York, 1986

In the course of her European career, Erika Giovanna Klien
was enrolled in Franz Cizek's art classes at the Vienna
Kunstgewerbeschule in 1918. She excelled under her
instructor's philosophy of letting his students develop at
their own pace. As tokens of esteem Cizek made Klien his
assistant and had eight of her drawings reproduced in his
educational manual, *Rochowanski 1922*. Klien came to the
attention of Katherine Dreier in 1926, while Dreier was on
an organizing trip for the Société Anonyme. Dreier was
interested in selecting some examples of student work from
Cizek's school for the Brooklyn International. Ultimately,
Klien was the only student from the Vienna school to show
in this prestigious forum.

Klien emigrated to the United States in 1929. After
settling in New York, she taught classes at the innovative
New School for Social Research, where she promoted her
mentor's conceptions and his enthusiasm for imagination
unfettered by definitive objectives and expectations. In a
brochure describing an art class she taught in 1935–36 she
wrote:

> The object of this course is to reawaken in the adult the
> capacity for rhythmic creation. No attempt is made to incul-
> cate any particular style but great emphasis is placed upon
> the relation of the students' work to contemporary forces.

Klien taught later at both the Dalton School and the
Spence School, eventually chairing the department of art at
the Walt Whitman School until her death in 1957.

Tower Caving In/Ober St. Viet of 1922 reflects Cizek's
conception of Kinetismus, which he defined as the " 'awaken-
ing of the eye' to the dynamism of contemporary life"
(Herbert, 390). Using a Cubist vocabulary, Klien articulates
the tower into multiple planes. She then animates the im-
mobile building, portrayed in static, typically Cubist forms,
with the dynamism of Futurist theory, utilizing a cascade of
dark and light tones. The monumentality of the tower is
barely contained within the limits of the picture plane,
effecting an implicit tension. This contradictory work trans-
forms an immovable object into one of energy and force.

S.V.

DER EINSINKENDE TVRM / OBER ST / VEIT -   ERIKA GIOVANNA KLIEN / 1922 -

Nina Osipovna Kogan

Russian, 1887–1942(?)

Suprematist Composition   1920–21
Tempera on canvas, 35 × 25¾ (88.9 × 65.4)
Provenance: Galerie Gmurzynska, Cologne, 1985

Very little is known about Nina Kogan, a second-generation Russian Suprematist painter. She was in charge of the preparatory classes at the Popular Art Institute in Vitebsk, which was directed by Marc Chagall. Kazimir Malevich's arrival at the institute in 1919 created a philosophical change that was ultimately responsible for Chagall's departure; Kogan stayed on. That same year she became involved in the Unovis group (Union of New Art, later Affirmers of the New Art), which was organized by Malevich. This group aimed "to fuse art with life" (Bowlt, 1988, 152).

In November of 1920 Kogan wrote in her essay "On Graphics in the Unovis Programme" that "the basis of the programme for the new school of art, Unovis, is a liberation from the slavish imitation of things and a training that teaches the student to operate with real pictorial, 'painterly' elements." She identified this philosophy as specifically Suprematist. Quoting her mentor, Malevich, Kogan said, "Everything is composed or constructed of straight lines, curves, volumes, and planes" which make up "the organism." The artist must examine this "construction" of elements and, in so doing, can explain "how things are built up and what they consist of" (Kogan, 163).

Kogan's *Suprematist Composition* was created at the time her essay was published and embodies the Unovis philosophy. It is composed of the basic visual elements identified by Malevich, that is, straight lines, curves, volumes, and planes. In addition, Kogan had noted that "all of nature" is constructed color, and indeed color plays an important role in this work; here it functions as a contributing element that helps to "organize the whole body" (Kogan, 163).

E.B.

Käthe Schmidt Kollwitz

German, 1897–1945

Prisoners Listening to Music   1925
Lithograph, 15⅞ × 14⅛ (39.7 × 35.8)
Provenance: Weyhe Gallery, New York; gift from Dannie
Rosenfield, 1973

In *Prisoners Listening to Music,* two men are shown in
attitudes of deep concentration. The lower of the two is
hunched over with his face tilted up, eyes wide open, lips
closed, as if in wonder. The higher figure rests his right arm
on the lower man's head and, in another gesture of intense
concentration, leans his chin on his huge hand, which
obscures his mouth. His ear is large, his cheek bones are
prominent, and his hair clings to his skull. The two men
seem oblivious of each other.

One of Kollwitz's methods of eliciting visual drama from
a subject was to represent the same thing in different ways
so as to give a fuller, more complete whole. In *Prisoners
Listening to Music* she compares two ways of listening. The
lower figure with his open face is directed outward, while
the upper figure, with his emphasized ear, seems locked
within himself. Kollwitz's subjects are far from our everyday experience, and this image of prisoners listening to
music evokes thoughts and questions of how they must feel.
Is this a concert in prison, or do they hear a parade going
by? What memories does this music stir in them? Is this
moment a release, a transcendence of pain?

The compositional and emotional focus achieved by Kollwitz in this lithograph was not spontaneous. In the first
state of the print three figures were drawn, two above and
one below, but the figure on the left, which stared out at
the viewer from deep, dark eye sockets, was eliminated after
early proofs. The third figure tended to diffuse and compli-
cate the image, which required greater simplicity. Nevertheless, some viewers of the second state have at first inter-
preted the right shoulder of the upper man as part of the
head of a third figure, seen just behind the head of the
lower man.

Kollwitz used both the ends and the sides of her litho
crayon in a drawing style that is at once gestural and
economical. (The texture of the crayon strokes makes it
apparent that Kollwitz used transfer lithography, which is
distinguished by the fact that the crayon marks appear to
catch the ridges of the paper on which it was originally
drawn, not those of a grained stone.) Every mark has a
function in building the image. She produced a full range of
darks and lights in a drawing that is essentially linear. The
strongest darks are in the eye sockets and nostrils, the
strongest lights on the tip of the nose and lower lip. Kollwitz uses the side of the litho crayon to delineate the
shoulder in powerful strokes.

A.W.

50

Lee Krasner
(Lenore Krassner)
American, 1908–1984

Black and White Collage   1953
Collage and oil on paper, 30 × 22⅜ (76.2 × 56.8)
Provenance: Mrs. Donald Braider, Sag Harbor, New York;
Robert Miller Gallery, New York, 1985

The background Lee Krasner brought to her intense in-
volvement in collage from 1951 to 1953 has been traced by
Barbara Rose. Krasner made her first collage painting in
1939, during her years as a WPA artist and a student at
Hans Hofmann's school. She created *Mosaic Collage* by
transforming an earlier work on paper, pasting a cut-paper
circle, a floral shape, and little rectangles and squares reminiscent of Mondrian onto the expressionistically painted and
intensely saturated painting.

Krasner had allied herself with a splinter group from the
Hofmann school, the American Abstract Artists, which was
fairly dogmatic in its rejection of subject matter, preferring
the geometric abstraction of artists such as Mondrian.
When Mondrian arrived in New York in 1940 he became a
friend of Krasner's, praising her for the sense of rhythm in
her painting. At this time, she and other artists were trying
to reconcile various currents of modernism, including nonobjective painting, abstraction, surrealism, and the intuitive
expressionism taught by Hofmann. Ultimately, this would
result in the complex style known as Abstract Expressionism. During the 1940s she evolved as a painter, and with
the energizing influence of Jackson Pollock (whom she
married in 1945) gradually freed herself from the intellectual
control inherited from Cubism to arrive at a far more
expressive, intuitive, and improvisational yet still disciplined
manner of working. During the war years, her experience
as a supervisor of exhibitions that encouraged participation
in the war effort gave her additional experience in collage
technique, cutting and pasting diverse materials to create
displays.

Krasner had admired Henri Matisse since her studies with
Hofmann. She saw Matisse's 1949 exhibition of cut-paper
works at Pierre Matisse Gallery, which inspired her, some
two years later, to begin to make a new type of collage
drawing/painting by tearing her own works on paper or

canvas and reassembling them. The torn edge interjected a
linear element that did not come from drawing but from a
physical act of destruction. Out of her destruction of her
own past came the creation of an extraordinary new
imagery.

Black and White Collage comes from the period when
Krasner was consistently exploring the collage medium
through a series of mostly black and white painted paper
works. In this collage, a violent clashing of forms results
from the juxtaposition and layering of drawn, cut, and
painted elements. There seem to have been two source
drawings that were combined, each contributing different
types of shapes, lines, and colors. Both were painted on the
same thick white paper, which has darkened and now
strongly contrasts with the broad strokes of thick white oil
overpainting. The interplay of black and white is rich and
complex, and consists of the following elements: white
(yellowed) paper shapes outlined in black; white oil paint
shapes or strokes over inky wet black paint; black shapes
with white torn paper edges; one mixed grey (black wash
over white paint); black dry brush; thumbtack holes; and
cast shadows from the three or more layers of paper. All of
this is enlivened by minute orange flecks.

This collage is like a puzzle in reverse; it seems that with
careful study one could reconstruct the process of its
creation. By means of the literal destruction of the older
drawings and their incorporation into a new, more vital
whole, Krasner achieved a critical breakthrough in her
work that was pivotal for the development of her art. She
was soon able to carry these ideas over into her paintings,
producing new works on canvas that were themselves collages, or others in which the painted image itself referred to
collage.

A.W.

52

Lois Lane
American, born in 1948

Snake   1981
Aquatint and etching, 15⅝ × 19½ (39.7 × 49.5)
Provenance: Signet Arts, St. Louis, 1982

Lois Lane's work was included in the 1979 exhibition "New Image Painting" at the Whitney Museum of American Art. The term "New Image" was applied to a group of artists who used realistic, figurative forms as elements of abstraction but retained some of the meaning of the figuration. Lane, who painted isolated, minimalized objects on arbitrary, monochromatic backgrounds, preserved or extended the meaning of her figurative elements while emphasizing formal, abstract concerns. Her black paintings contained familiar objects, such as doll dresses, masks, birds, orchids, and snakes, which, transformed by their inclusion in these dark images, seemed to become mysterious, hermetic, and powerful symbols. The secretive quality was compounded by the fact that Lane chose not to give titles to her works. In 1983 she showed two paintings of snakes "which coiled sinuously. The snake in [the] untitled 'WG no. 147' seems to be disappearing into a whirlpool of pink, gray and black, to the point, indeed, where citing it as a snake is rather pointless" (Henry, 155).

In 1981, Lane made *Snake*, together with a companion print depicting a masklike form. These were included in a portfolio of four etchings published by Parasol Press the following year. They were printed by Patricia Branstead at Aeropress in editions of thirty-three, with twelve artist's proofs. In *Snake*, the deep blue aquatint background is richly worked with lines, gouges, and scraping. The snake, realized with watery spit bite and printed in black, does not have surface markings, but seems instead to be an x-ray of a decomposing embryo, all soft tissue and lumpy. Although the snake's tongue has been described as made of gold leaf applied by hand (Museum of Fine Arts, 150), it seems to be painted. At the time of publication of the snake and mask prints, Ronny Cohen wrote,

Lois Lane is an artist who knows how to make simple images—reduced to the graphic basics—speak in deeply emotive, personal and wonderfully sophisticated terms. These two hand-colored aquatints show Lane doing what she does best. Each print investigates the inextricable relationship between form and subject, which is at the heart of her vision and has also figured in her recent paintings. . . . A coiled snakelike form, mostly black in color with white highlights, is set against a rich blue-black background. Like the mask, this image is tinged with the special emotive vitality that comes from the selective treatment of black as value, color and texture. The presentation, in which the horizontally disposed, rectangular plate appears to float within the space of a much larger, vertically disposed white sheet, plays up the iconic qualities in the black-dominated images. (Cohen, 102–3)

The loose handling of *Snake* reflects the artist's growing interest in her materials. Sarah Cecil noted, in a description that could also include Lane's use of etching, that by 1985 her paintings showed

more enjoyment of the painting process. The surfaces change from flat to glossy, from opaque to transparent. Wisps of a liquid gray, which seem to have been painted with smoke, blend and dissipate into the deep, dark ground. This liquid, tropical quality is appealing for its richness and mystery. (Cecil, 137)

A.W.

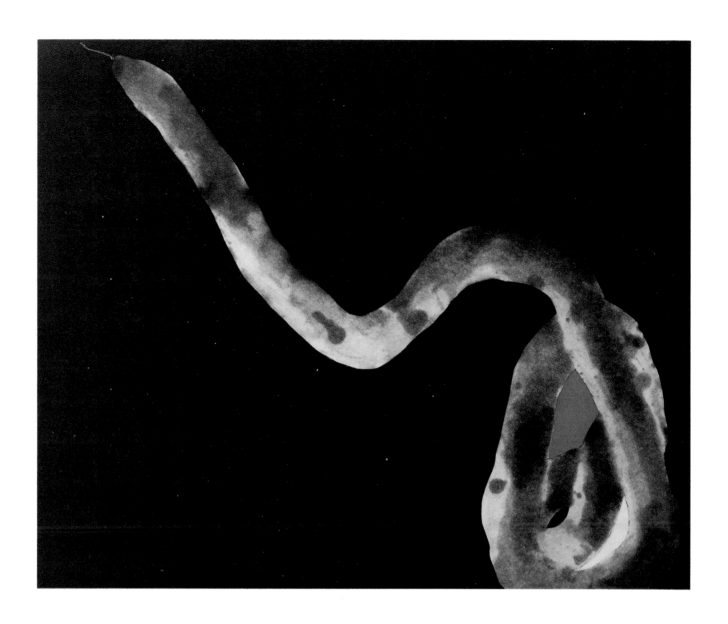

Edith Lawrence

English, 1890–1973

Cottage in the Woods   circa 1930
Linocut, 9⅝ × 11¾ (24.4 × 29.8)
Provenance: Wingrove Fine Prints, Washington, D.C., 1988

Edith Lawrence was a member of the Grosvenor School, a somewhat provincial art circle that prevailed in England between the wars. The group, consisting of Claude Flight and his students at the Grosvenor School of Modern Art, took up a relatively new and straightforward printmaking medium, the linocut. Lawrence's works, and those of the group as a whole, combined the formal elements of prewar Cubism and wartime Vorticism in the depiction of the rapid pace of modern life. Stressing form over content, and immaculate technique, the group was seen as apolitical and optimistic in the face of the political turmoil that engulfed Europe in the thirties. The "movement . . . was popular not only because it was good art, but because it made its fairly conservative public feel daring. The work was slightly shocking, but still legible, concurrently termed 'ultra-modern' and praised for making 'no undue demands' on its public" (Urbanelli, 19).

Lawrence and Flight were companions from the time of their meeting in 1920 until his death in 1955. Lawrence began her studies in art before they met, attending the Slade School between 1910 and 1914, and exhibiting paintings at the Royal Academy and the New English Art Club in 1916. A joint interest in the English arts and crafts movement led Lawrence and Flight to form an interior design business in which they employed the linocut process in textile and graphic design.

Together with Flight, Lawrence wrote and illustrated (in linocut) three children's books that provide a lighthearted pictorial survey of historical and cultural events: *A Little About Art, A Little About Geography,* and *A Little About History.* Her philosophy of art is reflected in a statement from *A Little About Art,* which stresses the importance of form over substance, stating that art need not have any subject other than its own balance, rhythm, and harmony (Lawrence, 31).

J.C.

Blanche Lazzell
American, 1878–1956

Petunias   1938
Monotype, 13⅝ × 11⅞ (34.6 × 30.2)
Provenance: Christie's, New York, September 12, 1985, sale
no. 5948

Blanche Lazzell is recognized as one of the leading members of the Provincetown Printers, a group which originated the single-block color woodcut process that has been termed the "Provincetown print." Having earned degrees in literature and art history, she began her study of studio arts in 1907 with classes taught by William Merritt Chase at the Art Students League. As was the case with many American artists she traveled to Paris, where she studied at the Académie Moderne in 1912–13. She left Europe following the outbreak of World War I, taking up residence in the burgeoning artists' colony at Provincetown, Massachusetts.

For forty years between 1916 and 1956, she spent most summers and occasional winters in Provincetown, creating more than 138 woodblocks and an undetermined number of impressions. In the one-block method the entire composition is carved onto a single block of wood and each color is separately inked and printed. Lazzell seldom made consistent editions and approached each subsequent printing as a unique experience. "Each print taken from the block is an individual work. . . . The creative faculty of the artist does not repeat; hence in the color print there are no exact duplicates" (Clarkson, 8). And, as she wrote to Katherine McCormick, "I use perfect freedom as to color and values. . . . I trust to my inspiration at the time I do the print" (Flint, 20).

Lazzell has been aptly described as "outwardly conservative" (Evual, 59). In fact hers was an adventurous spirit; she enjoyed experimentation and remained open to new experiences and ideas throughout her long career. She returned to Paris after the war, studying with Fernand Léger, Albert Gleizes, and André Lhote in 1923–24. Following the tenets of Cubism and Purism, she produced her most abstract works: still lifes of tabletops and guitars depicted in flat, unmodulated color planes that rotate and overlap each other. Her woodblock prints of 1923 and after, while more traditionally three-dimensional and representational than her paintings, echo the paintings in the use of flat planes of color and geometric simplification. Her works were included in the Salon d'Automne between 1923 and the mid-1930s, and in "L'Art d'aujourd'hui," the 1925 Parisian exhibition of the international avant-garde.

Lazzell enjoyed adapting subjects to different media. Although she is recognized almost exclusively for her woodblock prints, she worked extensively in other media, often taking a subject from watercolor to block print to monotype, oil, or (for a short period in the late 1920s, when she made hooked rugs) to fiber.

The Noun Collection monotype, executed in 1938 — the year in which Lazzell turned fifty years old and began studies with Hans Hofmann at his Provincetown School — is one of a number of studies of flowers, petunias in particular, done in monotype or woodblock print. She often used oil paints when making monotypes, and is said to have enjoyed the textural qualities achieved by this process (Clarkson, 38). The attention given to texture, modulated color, and painterly brushstroke in *Petunias* is quite unlike anything seen in Lazzell's woodblock prints and Cubist paintings.

Lazzell's subjects, often gleaned from her surroundings, included the buildings and wharves of Provincetown and the flowers from her "garden of boxes." She was an avid gardener, and her Provincetown studio, built at the end of a wharf, was surrounded by flowers growing in nail kegs and boxes and climbing fishing nets or strands of twine up to the roof. True to her modernist training she considered these subjects mere props for expression:

> To appreciate art of any period, we must dismiss the idea that painting is a representation of natural form as seen with the eye. Natural forms may be used as a means to expression, but never as an end in itself. . . . In a painting the aesthetic creation is primary; the subject matter, secondary. (Clarkson, 10)

J.C.

Petunias — Blanche Lazzell — 1938

Agnes Martin
American, born in 1921

The Garden   1958
Painted wood, 53 × 10 × 2 (134.6 × 25.4 × 5.1)
Provenance: Betty Parsons Foundation; Christie's, New
York, November 13, 1986, sale no. 6242, lot no. 284

Since the early 1960s Agnes Martin has been recognized as
an innovative artist whose most important works are her
large square canvases of delicate grids penciled on subtly
colored fields. While these particular paintings—works of
"delicacy and strength, toughness and loveliness" (Linville,
72)—are widely recognized, Martin's evolution as an artist
in the late 1940s and 1950s was characterized by discipline
and constant experimentation. Martin actually developed
her grid system gradually, over the course of a decade. Early
in this period, she worked in a style reminiscent of the biomorphic abstraction of Gottlieb and Baziotes. Later, she
abandoned the suggestion of organic form and three-dimensional space for the frontality and monumentality of
Rothko's loosely connected geometric forms. Finally, by the
mid to late 1950s, she gave up the romantic aspects of
abstract art for a more ordered, controlled, and detached
approach to geometric shapes upon the plane (Borden,
38–41).

Around 1956 (thanks to Betty Parsons), Martin, then
living in New Mexico, returned to New York, where she
had earlier attended Columbia University. In the city she
took a studio in the waterfront area known as Coenties Slip,
at the southern tip of Manhattan. Her neighbors included
Ellsworth Kelly and Jack Youngerman (who also exhibited
with Parsons), as well as Robert Indiana, James Rosenquist,
Charles Hinman, Lenore Tawney, Ann Wilson, and others.
While the artists of Coenties Slip did not share a mutual
style, their work had a number of elements in common, as
Stephanie Barron has noted. These included a nonpainterly
technique and a limited or monochromatic use of color.
Several of the painters, including Martin, Kelly, and
Indiana, made constructions out of found objects. Furthermore, Martin, Tawney, and Wilson (the three women of
the group) prefigured two future developments of New

York art—the minimalist organization of the grid and the
feminist aesthetic of craft media and techniques (Barron, 82).

Although Martin did not produce many constructions at
Coenties Slip, *The Garden*—an object made of a "found"
door and doorknobs—is closely related to her paintings of
the period, which are geometric, frontal, and limited in
color (Borden, 42; Ashton, 8). Like many of Martin's
paintings that draw their inspiration from the land, the title
alludes to the earth, in this case to a tilled field upon which
mushroomlike organisms grow. *The Garden* seems totemic,
rigid, and frontal, yet it is also an extremely whimsical and
poetic work. In fact, *The Garden* does not "represent" the
earth (any more than Mondrian's Neoplasticist paintings
signify "landscape"). Martin's titles, as Lawrence Alloway
has noted, while "not openly descriptive . . . are persistently
evocative; they have a definite congruence to the artist's
visual imagery" (Alloway, 10).

H.F.

Berthe Morisot
French, 1841–1895

Self-portrait with Daughter (The Drawing Lesson)
circa 1888–90
Drypoint on thin laid paper, 7 × 5⅛ (17.8 × 13.0)
Provenance: Joseph Faulkner Main Street Galleries,
Chicago, 1984

Berthe Morisot, one of the original Impressionists, made a total of twelve drypoints and one lithograph, all of which she executed between 1888 and 1891. She is thought to have begun making prints because Stéphane Mallarmé had asked her to contribute an illustration to a book of his poems. Mary Cassatt may have provided technical guidance (Stuckey, 128–30). This impression of *Self-portrait with Daughter* is one of a few rare artist's proofs pulled prior to Ambroise Vollard's acquisition and publication of small editions of Morisot's drypoints in Paris around 1900. Vollard probably omitted the four other plates because of the lightness of line in those drypoints, leading Delteil and others to state that eight prints was the sum total of Morisot's production (Johnson, 137–8). Morisot lightly inscribed the drypoint marks on her copper plates, raising just enough burr to catch ink and give a soft, velvety richness to the line. She drew with many short, curving strokes, and her construction lines are evident. Of her graphic output, Roger Passeron wrote:

> These eight drypoints confirm the high distinction and feminine delicacy of Berthe Morisot's style, but they do not have the astonishing firmness and sureness of line that we find in Mary Cassatt. (Passeron, 132)

Passeron compares the delicate "feminine" work of Morisot to the only other woman Impressionist, yet Cassatt had her own stylistic sources, especially the vigorous linear prints of the eighteenth-century Japanese artist Utamaro. It therefore makes more sense to compare the lightness of line in Morisot's prints with that seen in the work of other artists of the first Impressionist group, such as Pissarro, Renoir, her brother-in-law and friend Edouard Manet, or even with Whistler.

In her essay on Morisot's *Wet Nurse with Julie* of 1879 Linda Nochlin discusses images of work in Impressionist painting. Her points are applicable to the drypoint *Self-portrait with Daughter*. She notes that many images of women's work (including nursing, bartending, entertaining, prostitution, and painting) have been considered scenes of middle-class leisure rather than of women earning a living. Morisot's painting depicts a wet nurse nursing the artist's newborn daughter, Julie Manet. Both the wet nurse and the painter were producing products for profit—milk and art. Morisot's conflicting roles as mother and professional artist (mutually exclusive, by the standards of her contemporaries) clearly influenced her imagery. Nochlin says that *Wet Nurse's*

> stimulating ambiguities may have as much to do with the contradictions involved in contemporary mythologies of work and leisure, and the way that ideologies of gender intersect with these paired notions, as they do with Morisot's personal feelings and attitudes. (Nochlin, 39)

Despite Morisot's personal feelings of conflict, the affection of mother and child, as well as the artist's success in integrating art and motherhood, are communicated clearly in Morisot's many pictures of her daughter.

Julie Manet, born in 1878, would have been eleven or twelve years old at the time Morisot made *Self-portrait with Daughter*. The drypoint shows Morisot on a divan, holding a piece of paper. She is looking outward, away from the drawing. Julie, who is standing, leans on her mother's shoulder. She rests one hand on the couch arm and looks attentively at the drawing her mother is holding. Although this print is known by an alternate title, "The Drawing Lesson," it is surely not the child who has made the drawing but the mother. Otherwise the mother would be looking at the child's artwork. The mother is looking out because she is in the process of making the drawing that was the basis for this self-portrait print. Morisot depicts herself in her simultaneous roles as working artist and mother. The print is related to a sanguine drawing made in 1888, *Berthe Morisot with Julie, Sketching,* which depicts the artist-mother drawing and her daughter looking at the art work. In the drawing Julie is looking over her mother's shoulder and her hand is reaching out to touch her mother. Around this time Morisot made an undated drawing of a girl about the same age, in which the child is holding a sketch pad. Her whole family was much involved in drawing, for she had also made a painting of her husband, Eugène Manet, sketching while playing with Julie (Nochlin, 50), who was to become a favorite model for Renoir.

A.W.

Gabriele Münter

German, 1877–1962

Laundry at the Beach   circa 1907–08
Linocut, 5⅞ × 9½ (14.9 × 24.1)
Provenance: Allan Frumkin Gallery, Chicago; George M.
Irwin, Quincy, Illinois, 1983

In 1916, just prior to the dissolution of their fifteen-year relationship, Wassily Kandinsky wrote of Gabriele Münter:

> She is bound by the contemplative, immediate, one is tempted to say, by the innocent feeling for nature and the world. Gabriele Münter was receptive to every artistic influence and understood not only French art, but also that of other countries and other epochs, but in spite of this understanding she has remained herself, and her work is quite unmistakable. (Jacob, 104)

August Macke had probably come closer to the essence of Münter's inspiration when, five years earlier, he postulated that the painter was "strongly drawn to the mysterious," and that there was something inherently "German" in her romanticism (Jacob, 106). In her mature works, Münter was able to integrate her awareness of international modernist tendencies with her appreciation of and familiarity with local Bavarian folk traditions, in particular with *Hinterglasmalerie* (painting on verso of glass), which she avidly collected and occasionally executed. The lyrical poetic primitivism evident in her paintings of 1908 to 1914, for which she is best known, epitomize the aesthetic, mystical expression of romantic self inherent in the goals of the loosely knit Blaue Reiter (Blue Rider) circle, of which she was a founding member. Unlike the work of those members of the group who embraced nonobjective art, Münter's work always remained representational and, as a result, maintained its overt reference to one of her primary sources, the paintings and objects of local "naive" peasant artists, wherein she had identified a primal integration of man, nature, and the universe.

Gabriele Münter's early academic training was in Düsseldorf, where she studied with a local painter and took classes at the Ladies' Art School. Disillusioned with the limitations she encountered in her studies, she traveled to America in 1897, returning to Germany in 1900 and in 1901 she began studies at the Munich Association of Women Artists, an institution under the influence of the *Jugendstil* (Youth Style) movement. In 1902, a pivotal year in Münter's life, she entered the newly established Phalanx school and began working with Kandinsky, who was the school director and president of the internationally minded Phalanx group. Münter attended Kandinsky's summer class in Kochel in 1902 and another in Kallmünz the following summer during which time the two became engaged. In 1904, Münter and Kandinsky began their travels to Tunisia, Italy, France, and throughout Germany, in the course of which they became thoroughly familiar with the work of Rousseau, Picasso, and the French Fauves. Münter and Kandinsky exhibited their work in Paris at both the Salon d'Automne and the Salon des Indépendants of 1907. In 1908 they settled in Munich and the following year Münter purchased her own house in Murnau; her home became a gathering place for members of the New Artists Federation, which Kandinsky and Alexei von Jawlensky (both of whom were Russian émigrés) founded in 1909, and to which Münter would belong, and after 1911, for her fellow members of the Blaue Reiter circle.

It was Jawlensky who introduced Münter to Bavarian glass painting in 1908 and to Rambold, a local folk artist under whose tutelage she learned to make them. Münter's experiments with *Hinterglasmalerie* were instrumental in the development of her mature style, which employed black outlines and broad swatches of intense, symbolic, almost magical, nonrepresentational color. However, a second means by which she achieved her unmistakable fluency was the woodcut medium.

Münter's first encounter with the woodcut occurred in 1902 while she was a student at the Phalanx school. She returned to the medium in 1906, and through it developed a means of working that allowed her to set down bold black outlines and broad color planes, two attributes of her later painting. Despite its overtly naturalistic references, the linoleum cut *Laundry at the Beach,* hints at the change that is about to take place in Münter's style. Through its juxtaposition of black line, abstract color planes, and almost overpoweringly strong black forms alongside careful renderings of the details of everyday realities, the piece stands as strong evidence of a transitional phase of the artist's oeuvre.

E.M.

Gabriele Münter
German, 1877–1962

House with Fir Trees in the Snow   circa 1938
Oil on board, 39⅛ × 28 (99.4 × 71.1)
Provenance: Dalzell Hatfield Galleries, Los Angeles;
Virginia Steele Scott, Pasadena; Christie's, New York,
October 21, 1980, sale no. 5012, lot no. 36

From 1909 until the outbreak of the First World War,
Gabriele Münter's house in Murnau, where she and Wassily
Kandinsky spent a good deal of their time, was a gathering
place for members of the avant-garde, including August
Macke, Franz Marc, Paul Klee, and the Russian expatriates
Alexei von Jawlensky and Marianne von Werefkin, who
had emigrated with Kandinsky to Germany in 1896. As her
paintings from the period indicate, these years were among
the most productive of Münter's career. By 1910, her
mature, fluent style was well in place, her works were
imbued with unquestioned sureness and magnitude of
vision, and her colors were clear, nonrepresentational,
powerful, and magical. In 1911 she, Kandinsky, and Marc
withdrew from the New Artists Federation. On December 18
of that year the first Blaue Reiter (Blue Rider) exhibition
opened at the Thannhauser Gallery and, in 1912, the only
issue of the anthology *Der Blaue Reiter* appeared. Unlike the
German Expressionist group Die Brücke (The Bridge),
whose works they included in their shows, the Blaue Reiter
artists were less committed to social commentary and criticism than to the spiritual expression of self. Furthermore,
unlike Die Brücke, the participants in the Blaue Reiter were
never formally consolidated into a structured community.
The closest that the circle would ever come to such communal experience took place during Münter's regular artists'
open houses in the Alpine village of Murnau. By 1913, the
movement ceased, for all intents and purposes, to exist.

The outbreak of hostilities in 1914 forced both Münter
and Kandinsky to flee Germany. Kandinsky returned to
Russia and Münter relocated in Stockholm. Although they
saw each other occasionally during the next few years, they
separated permanently in the spring of 1916. Münter did not
resume her residence in Murnau until 1931. During the
intervening years her style shifted abruptly, and during the

1920s she nearly abandoned her art-making activities,
producing very little. Münter began painting again in
earnest in the 1930s only to have her work classified as
degenerate by the Nazis and removed from the Munich Art
Association in 1937. The artist spent the years until the end
of World War II in her house, secretly painting at night.
As works such as *House with Fir Trees in the Snow* illustrate,
she rediscovered her unmistakable vision at that time.

Münter had first experienced the freedom of painting out
of doors in 1902 as a young student of Kandinsky's, during
a summer school class. That same summer she learned to
use the palette knife to express her emotional responses to
the environment quickly and directly. The tracks of the
palette knife are clearly evident in the Noun Collection
painting. So too are Münter's fluency with nonrepresentational color, her compositional prowess, and her fascination
with the formal ramifications of the familiar cloisonné-like,
bold, dark outline, which she mastered only some years
after her summer school experience. The landscape is far
more mysterious, however, than are most of the paintings
of her Blaue Reiter period. That such is the case is under-
standable when one considers that this is a painting of day
that was executed at night; a depiction of the recollection,
not only of the natural light that is no longer available to
the eye, but also of the experience of painting, and living,
en plein air no longer accessible to the spirit.

                                                    E.M.

Agnes Pelton
American, 1881–1961

Ecstasy   1928
Oil on canvas, 23⅝ × 18¾ (60.0 × 47.6)
Provenance: The artist; private collection, California;
Richard York Gallery, New York, 1988

Agnes Pelton has until recently received little attention from scholars. However, the most comprehensive source about her, the recent catalogue of the inaugural exhibition of the National Museum of Women in the Arts, has begun to redress this oversight, and her innovative works will surely be more widely recognized in the future (Tufts, no. 80).

Born in Stuttgart to American parents, Pelton grew up in France and Switzerland before obtaining her art degree from the Pratt Institute in Brooklyn in 1900. Following a year in Italy, Pelton returned to New York and studied with Arthur Wesley Dow, William Langson Lathrop, and Hamilton Easter Field. Pelton was active professionally in these years. She contributed two paintings to the Armory Show in New York in 1913; in 1915 she participated in the Women's Suffrage Exhibition at Macbeth Galleries and received honorable mention for *Philosophy,* her submission to Mrs. Harry Payne Whitney's contest for mural decoration; and in 1917 she was included in a group exhibition of the Knoedler Galleries. Pelton was a member of several artists' societies, including the Associated Artists of Long Island, the American Federation of Arts, and the National Association of Women Painters and Sculptors, for whom she served as recording secretary in 1917 (Opitz, 712). During the 1910s and 1920s she traveled and exhibited widely: In 1919 she showed pastels of Taos in Santa Fe; she spent time in the mid-twenties painting in the Hawaiian Islands; and in 1926 she journeyed to the Middle East (Tufts, no. 80).

Following these trips, Pelton moved away from the figurative art of her earlier landscapes, portraits, and flower studies toward a more abstract style. *Ecstasy,* painted in 1928, was included in two important exhibitions of 1929 that featured her new works—"Decorative Flower Painting and Abstractions," held at the Grace Nicholson Art Galleries in Pasadena, California, and "Abstractions by Agnes Pelton," held at the Montross Gallery in New York. The titles of the new paintings at the Montross Gallery exhibition—such as *The Fountains, Incarnation, Caves of the Mind,* and *Sleep*—reflect Pelton's more abstract approach. In February 1931 *Ecstasy* was exhibited again at the Argent Galleries in New York. The show was reviewed in *Art News.* The magazine's critic paraphrased the catalogue introduc-

tion written by the composer and philosopher Dane Rudyhar: Rudyhar characterized Pelton's abstractions as having "both actual being as entities of a semi-subjective world and universal significance as impersonal symbols of human experience. . . . Each painting is a compelling word of tongue that everyone may understand who for a moment draws within his [*sic*] or herself and tunes in with the universally living stream of living experience." The critic concluded, "In the trend away from materialism in general, and from literalism in art in particular, Miss Pelton is a child of the new age. She is harbinger of the future for other painter poets" ("Calendar of Exhibitions," 10).

That the critic noted Pelton's role as painter and poet is appropriate, for the artist composed verses to accompany *Ecstasy:*

> In a rush of Ecstasy
> A flower bursts
> To meet the day—
> Its petals bent
> So sudden its release
>
> Gray shapes that pressed
> Harrassed the once blind bud
> When from below
> Pushed up the menace
> Of a hook of darkness,
> Swift and free
> The life force gathered
> And opened to the light.

Using color and form symbolically, Pelton's *Ecstasy* is no ordinary botanical specimen but a sonorous emblem of growth. As Pelton herself perhaps wrote in the introduction to the catalogue for her first show of abstractions in 1929:

> Here color is like a voice, giving its message directly, without translation into the presentment of recognizable colored objects. Like music without an instrument, it acts on the perception which is sympathetically ready to receive it; but as the creative faculty acts in building forms, the colors active here produce forms in space according to their nature and the quality of life which they represent. (Tufts, no. 80)

H.F.

Liubov Sergeevna Popova

Russian, 1889–1924

Spatial Force Construction   circa 1921–22
Gouache, ink, and graphite, 16 × 11⅜ (41.0 × 28.9)
Provenance: Gift of the artist to Joseph Popovits, spring
1922; by descent to his son; George Peck, New York;
Rachel Adler Gallery, New York, 1986

Liubov Popova was one of many Russian artists who used
their studies of Cubism in France as the basis for architectonic work created in the late teens through the twenties.
In 1912 Popova studied at La Palette, the atelier of Le
Fauconnier, Metzinger, and de Segonzac. There she met
several other Russian artists with whom she would later
work, including Nadezhda Udaltsova. By 1913 Popova was
back in Moscow, studying at Vladimir Tatlin's studio. John
Bowlt observes that during the war years her work evolved
from Synthetic Cubism to a nonfigurative art form (Bowlt,
81). In 1916 Popova rejected figurative painting altogether
and began working exclusively with architectonic forms.
She saw these works "not as independent units, but as
components of a new material — and hence new, spatial —
environment" (Bowlt, 81).

In September 1921 Popova participated in the "5 × 5 = 25"
exhibition along with Alexandra Exter, Alexandr Rod-
chenko, Varvara Stepanova, and Alexandr Vesnin. After the
show she "practically gave up studio work," stating that
"our activity as pure painters is purposeless." Instead she
turned to stage and textile design. Bowlt suggests that the
titles of works such as *"Painterly-Force Compositions, Space-
Volume, Color Planes, Enclosed Spatial Construction,* [and]
Space-Force . . . demonstrate her new appreciation of space."
The theatrical producer Vsevolod Meierkhold saw in
Popova's works the strong potential for "an extra-theatrical
spectacle." Meierkhold's frequent visits to the show led to
his inviting Popova to create a course program at his State
Higher Producer Workshops. Although it is not known
whether *Spatial Force Construction* appeared in "5 × 5 = 25"
or at the time of her designs for Meierkhold's 1922
production of *The Magnanimous Cuckold,* Louis Lozowick
does describe the stage design as being very sparse, with "a

simple, skeleton-like construction, a scaffolding designed by
Popova" (Bowlt, 86–87).

This description might be applied to the Popova gouache
in the Noun Collection, as well. The composition is made
only of diagonals. Bowlt remarks that the way in which
Popova cleans up the picture plane is very typical of her
work, "where she applies a method of rigid stratification,
i.e., the imposition of a grid of conflicting lines" (Bowlt,
85). Like most of the contemporary progressive artists in
Russia, Popova worked with similar themes regardless of
the particular medium. Her aim was to expose "the latent,
inner energy of form" (Rakitin, 200).

E.B.

Carla Prina

Swiss resident, born in Italy in 1911

TOP:
Composition   1941
Oil on wood, 7½ × 9 (19.0 × 22.9)
Provenance: The artist; Galerie Gmurzynska, Cologne, 1987

BOTTOM:
Composition   1943
Oil on wood, 6¼ × 8 (15.9 × 20.3)
Provenance: The artist; Galerie Gmurzynska, Cologne, 1987

The artists of modern Italy began to work in abstraction as early as the first decade of the twentieth century; the first examples were produced in accord with the chromatic and optical theories of Symbolism and Divisionism (Caramel, 187) and, a few years later, with the political aims of the Futurists. This latter group advocated the destruction of a culturally bankrupt Italy and proposed in their art and radical literature to create a dynamic new world of "aggressive motion, feverish insomnia, the swift pace, the fatal leap, the slap, and the punch" (Coen, 50).

After the horror of World War I, during which several major Futurist artists died and others left the movement, came a period of "return to order" in Italy. The remaining Futurists entered into a difficult dialogue with Mussolini and Fascism, all the while remaining in contact with the movements of the international avant-garde, including Constructivism, Neo-Plasticism, and the Bauhaus.

Although the left-wing anarchism of the earliest Futurists could not ultimately be reconciled with Mussolini's bureaucratic and absolutist regime, their work established and maintained a tradition of abstraction in Italy that was to flourish in the thirties. Crucial for its promotion was the Galleria del Milione in Milan, a bookshop/gallery; in 1934 it held the first exhibition of abstract Italian art and published the "Declaration of the Exhibitors" that became known as the manifesto of Italian abstraction. Among the artists associated with the gallery was a group from the city of Como, just north of Milan, who worked in close artistic dialogue with the architects of the Rationalist movement, Italy's version of the International Style.

The strains of Futurism, Italian abstraction, and Rationalist architecture merge in Carla Prina's work and personal life. Born in Como, Prina studied art at Milan's Brera Academy, in Greece, and at the French Academy in Rome. She traveled widely in Europe and began to exhibit in 1933. In the mid-thirties she joined the Como group. Among the affiliated Rationalist architects was Alberto Sartoris, whom Prina would marry in 1943. Ten years her senior, he had been associated with the Futurist movement in the 1920s, had maintained a long correspondence with the Dutch De Stijl artist Theo van Doesburg, and had exhibited with the artists of the Abstraction-Création group in Paris. Sartoris

became an enthusiastic and prolific supporter of Prina and has written several books and articles about her. (Indeed, Prina's work has inspired an extensive literature in Italian and French on her importance in the history of abstraction.)

Prina is often described as a last-generation Futurist, because she exhibited in the Futurist pavilion of the Venice Biennale in 1942, and in 1943 in the Futurist room of the Rome Quadriennale. But by then the political enthusiasm of the early Futurists had been replaced by efforts promoting abstraction, and Prina participated actively in exhibitions of abstract art.

The Rationalist architects had inspired the Como artists' group to consider issues of space, structure, and materials in their work, and Prina's interest in architectonic forms is readily visible in her art. The critic Carlo Belli, spokesman for the Galleria del Milione artists, felt that the architects "worked a miracle" among their artist colleagues. "Those forms, those new dimensions, created the need for an equivalent in the fine arts" (Caramel, 188). Artists and architects collaborated on a few projects; Prina herself painted the frescoes of the Prina Chapel in Sondrio. One critic suggested that hers is work "made for architecture, for the urban décor" (Seuphor, unp.).

The untitled Prina works in the Noun Collection were painted during the middle of the war years. Edmond Humeau has suggested that Prina's work disproves the axiomatic notion that the tragedies of an artist's environment are always reflected in her work. Her paintings, he said, recreate the "joy of exultant nature." He compared her technical facility to that of the painters of the Italian Renaissance, adding that her "delicate colors [are] brushed with a Venetian perfection" (Humeau, unp.). The Noun works use media more typical of the Renaissance than of modern art, oil on wood; their painterly tactile surfaces form a surprising, close-up contrast to the clean lines of their abstract forms.

G.Z.

Olga Vladimirovna Rozanova

Russian, 1886–1918

Directional Lines   1913
Oil on canvas, 39⅜ × 31 (100.0 × 78.7) (sight)
Provenance: Filippo Tommaso Marinetti, Rome; Leonard
Hutton Galleries, New York, 1979

In 1913, Olga Vladimirovna Rozanova proclaimed the "rise of a new era in creation" when she published her theoretical treatise "The Bases of the New Creativity and the Reasons for Its Misinterpretation" in *Soyuz molodezhi,* the publishing organ of the St. Petersburg-based Union of Youth group. She stated,

> Only modern art has advocated the full and serious importance of such principles as pictorial dynamism, volume equilibrium, weight and weightlessness, linear and plane displacement, rhythm as a legitimate division of space, design, plane, and surface dimension, texture, color correlation, and others. (Rozanova, 14–22).

The correlation between this statement and the dynamist landscape *Directional Lines* of 1913 is clear. Mikhail Larionov and Natalia Gontcharova's "Rayists and Futurists: A Manifesto," which appeared that same year, provides further commentary: "Rayist painting has in view spatial forms, arising from the intersection of reflected rays of various objects, forms chosen by the artist's will" (Lodder, 17; Leonard Hutton, 92).

The painting was first exhibited in St. Petersburg in late 1913 and early 1914, and, following Filippo Tommaso Marinetti's first Futurist tour of Russia, it was shipped to Italy for inclusion in the "Free Futurist International Exhibition of Painting and Sculpture" at the Galleria Sprovieri in April and May of 1914. *Directional Lines* was not destined to return to Russia but remained instead in Italy where it was eventually incorporated into Marinetti's private collection in Rome. Although *Directional Lines* is obviously about the fragmentation of objects and the spatial consequences of this violent disunion, it would be mistaken to assume that the work corresponds completely with Larionov and Gontcharova's elucidation of Rayist principles in their pure form. Unlike some of the paintings executed by the two as early as 1910 that ignore the object completely and concentrate upon the dynamism inherent to the intersection of light rays emanating from, and between, objects in space, Rozanova's painting retains its reference to concrete things — to tree, edifice, earth, and sky — and concentrates instead on their displacement. Furthermore, it would be a mistake to assume

that *Directional Lines* responded to the formulaic canons of Italian Futurism, with which Rozanova was thoroughly familiar, as were most of her fellow members of the early twentieth-century Russian avant-garde. What makes Rozanova's work undeniably her own, and inherently Russian, is its insistence upon the supremacy of individual feeling, intuition, and personal experience. It is precisely these qualities that imbue the painting with its honest power.

Throughout her brief career, Rozanova was involved in numerous acts of synthesis, dissolving boundaries not only between various artistic media, but also between visual language and its verbal equivalent, between rationality and intuition, between the fine arts and their industrial as well as vernacular counterparts. She participated in most of the major exhibitions of Russian avant-garde art of her period. Following her unexpected death from diphtheria in November 1918, a commemorative exhibition of her work was mounted in Moscow by the Visual Arts Section of the Commissariat for Enlightenment. The show was composed of 270 paintings and works on paper representative of the full range of her artistic experimentation. One cannot help but assume that, had she lived, she would have avoided falling prey to the complacencies of which she warned in her 1913 manifesto:

> Only the absence of honesty and of true love of art provides some artists with the effrontery to live on stale tins of artistic economics stocked up for years, and year in, year out, until they are fifty, to mutter what they had first talked about when they were twenty. . . . Contempt should be cast on those who hold dear only peaceful sleep and relapses into past experience. (Rozanova, 20–21)

E.M.

Olga V. Rozanova
Alexei E. Kruchenykh
Russian, 1886–1918 and 1885–1922

A Duck's Nest . . . of Bad Words   1913–14
23 lithographs with watercolor, approximately 4½ × 6⅞
(11.3 × 17.5) each
Provenance: Carus Gallery, New York, January 1987

One indigenous attribute of early twentieth-century Russian avant-garde works is their juxtaposition of opposites, of the logical and the illogical, the intuitive and the rational. Such counterbalance, or "counterpoint of ideas," is particularly evident in the works and writings of "the pioneers of abstraction—Wassily Kandinsky, Kazimir Malevich, and Olga Rozanova" (Bowlt, 221). Rozanova's nonobjective triumphs were precipitated by her experiments in the book art medium, in particular by her collaboration with the community of transrational poets of which she herself became an active member.

During the years 1904 through 1910, Rozanova attended the Bolshakov Art School and the Stroganov School of Applied Art in Moscow. In 1911 she moved to St. Petersburg and became a member of the Union of Youth, exhibiting with the group and contributing to its publications. While affiliated with this group she became acquainted with Kazimir Malevich and Alexei Kruchenykh. In 1912 she first began designing and executing Cubo-Futurist books.

For the Russian avant-garde painters and poets, the second decade of the twentieth century was a period of heady excitement and intense creative activity. In 1912, Kruchenykh, David Burliuk, and Vladimir Mayakovsky composed their manifesto, "A Slap in the Face of Public Taste." The tract was printed on toilet paper and circulated throughout Moscow. Futurist street events were mounted replete with outrageous costumes; artists paraded through the streets, their faces painted, sometimes in formal dress with spoons in their lapels, sometimes in a state of informal undress. Exhibitions, lectures, and publications followed one upon the other in a tumultuous fashion; new schools of poetry and painting were invented and proselytized. Cries rang through studio, gallery, and street in support of such concepts as intuition, displacement, disharmony, disconstruction, and construction.

In January of 1913, the poet Kruchenykh, with whom Rozanova would collaborate regularly and who would later become her husband, published his first *zaum,* or transrational poem (Bowlt, 225):

dyr bul shchyl
ubeshshchur
skum
vy so bu
r l ez

In April of that year he and Velimir Khlebnikov published "The Declaration of the Word as Such," the first *zaum* manifesto. For the poets, *zaum* was, at one and the same time, destructive and constructive. Searching for a universal language, they used displacement, intuition, and other deliberately alogical constructs to derive a vocabulary that would come closer to *true* meaning than could conventional linguistic systems. In collaboration with painters and other poets they produced works that, in their own words, appeared to have been "written and read in the twinkling of an eye (singing, splash, dance, throwing down of clumsy structures, forgetting, unlearning . . .)," as though "written with difficulty, more uncomfortable than blackened boots . . ." (Hilton, 34).

Collaborations such as Rozanova and Kruchenykh's 1913 *A Duck's Nest . . .* conform to these transrational principles. The work is further enhanced by the fact that the *zaum* text is handwritten, a device deliberately employed to further intensify the feeling of "twinkling," intuitive expression. Rozanova's lithographs and watercolors do not serve as illustrations for the poems but are instead parallel visual equivalents executed in response to similar concerns. Conversely, Khlebnikov's poetry cannot be viewed as a mere appendage to the prints and color washes. Text and image intertwine and speak as one. As is stated in the first *zaum* manifesto:

> Thought and speech cannot catch up with the emotional experience of someone inspired, the artist is free to express himself not only in a common language (concept), but also in a private one (a creator is individual), as well as in a language that does not have a definite meaning (is not frozen), that is *transrational.* A common language is binding; a free one allows more complete expression. (Bowlt, 225–26)

E.M.

Эф-луч.

Гудокъ раздавался все глуше
летящихъ погребу туш
Что кромѣ кузнецовъ
невѣдали отцовъ

Огоньи смрадихъ платья
Амолоты объятья
Палачъ чума сестра и братья

Быстролетѣли
Скорбечемъ разумъ
Ильсовѣсти ротозѣи
Разбивая древнія вазы

Одна вослѣдъ задругой
Уродяивоетѣло
И птичьими лапкамисѣла
Еврейской весело ногой

Схлыстами иростями люди
Здѣсь лазаливамъ
В ушастой простудѣ
Махали руками
Полывая уснувшій камень

Птица карапаетъ землю ногой
Палачъ для Яканова тащитъ черед
Вблизи шагалъ часовой
В шеб распухнувшій веред

Желѣзная няня сосцами
висячими
Кормила согбенныхъ цыплятъ

Усатыя с очками блестящими
Безмозглыхъ безмордыхъ телятъ
Нос сердца чумой настоящими

КЛОХТАЛИ ЦЫПЛЯТА В ПУХУ
ЗВЕНѢЛИ ИХ МѢДНЫЕ КЛЮВЫ
С МѢДНОЮ СИЛОЙ В ПАХУ
КРИЧАЛИ И ПѢЛИ УВЫ

БАБА ИЗ ГЛИНЫ ГЛАЗѢЛА
ТОЛСТАЯ СѢЛА КАК КРЯК
ИЗ РУБИЩА ПАДАЛО ТѢЛО
А ГЛАЗА УМЕРШІЙ ЧЕРВЯК

ЗВЕНѢЛИ ТРУДНЫЯ ПАСТИ
ПАУТИНОЙ КОРЯВЫЕ ПАЛЬЦЫ
И НА ГРУДИ ТОРЧАЛИ СЛАСТИ
ЖЕЛѢЗНЫЕ К ДѢВАМ СКИТАЛЬЦЫ

РѢСНИЦ РАЗВЕРЗАЛИСЬ ВѢНОЧКИ
И НА МАШИНѢ ЛЕТѢЛ ЭФ-ЛУЧ
КАК БУДТО В ОКНО ОДИНОЧКИ
ВЗОР УЗНИКА УЗОК И ЖГУЧ

КИДАЯ СТОЗУБОСТЬ ПЛЕВКА
КРОВЬ СОБИРАЯ В СОСУД
ВСЕ Д ОСТАВАЛА ХУДАЯ РУКА
НА ЛАДОНЬ УКЛАДАЯ МИНУТ

И ПАДАЛИ ЖЕРТВЫ СО СТОНОМ
ЗВЕНЯ МОСТОВОЙ О ЗАТЫЛОК
ПЕЧАЛЬСЬ О ПРЕЖНЕМ ИОНОМ
ДЛЯ МОЛНІЙ ПРАЗДЕН НАПИЛОК

В СѢ ПРОЧЬ ПОБѢЖАЛИ
КАК БУДТО ИХ ЖДАЛИ
КАК БУДТО БЫ ЗНАЛИ
О СМЕРТИ ПОЖАРѢ

И ТОЛЬКО ЗА ЛѢСОМ
МУЖЧИНЫ ОРАЛИ
НЕ ЗНАЯ О СБЫВШЕЙСЯ
ЛУЧИСТОЙ КАРѢ

О НАД ЗВѢЗДНОМ НА СЕРАѢ УДАРѢ

И ТОЛЬКО ЛЯГУШКИ ЗА ОЗЕРОМ
КРЯКАЛИ
И ПСЫ ЛИШ НАД ПЕПЛОМ ВЫЛИ
И ДѢВУШКИ В ПОСЛѢДНІЙ РАЗ ПЛАКАЛ
НАД КНИГОЮ ; ЛЮДИ КОГДА ТО ЗДѢСЬ
БЫЛИ

ГЛУПОСТИ РЫЖЕЙ ЖАЖДУ
И ЗАБВЕНІЯ ДАВНИХ ПУТЕЙ
БУДУ ДИК Я ДВАЖДЫ
КОЛЬ УБѢГУ
МЫСЛЕЙ

ПО ПОЛЮ ОГЛОХШИХ КАМНЕЙ
БУДУ СРЫВАТЬ ПЛЕВКОВ
ЦВѢТЫ
И НАДЕЖДЫ БОЛЬНЫМИ
РУКАМИ
СХВАЧУ РЕЗИНОВЫЙ ШИП
НЕВѢСТЫ
ИЛИ СЯДУ НА НАКОВАЛЬНЮ
И ПОСКАЧУ ГРОМЫХАЯ
И ПОДЫМЕТСЯ КРИК ЗАВА-
ЛЕННЫХ
И НЕ БУДУ ЗНАТЬ
МОЖЕТ ТАМ МАТЬ
РОДНАЯ...

Я ПЛЮНУЛ СМѢЛО НА РЕТИВЫХ
ПРИШЕДШИХ ОХРАНЯТЬ МОЙ
ПРАХ
—СКОЛЬКО СКОРБИ СЛЕЗЛИВОЙ
В ПОНУРЕННЫХ ГОЛОВАХ—

ПЛЕВОК ПУСКАЙ РАЗБУДИТ СИХ
А МНѢ НЕ НАДО ПЛАЧА
ЖИВУ В ВѢКАХ ИНЫХ
ВСЕГДА Я ЖИВУ.... КАК КЛЯЧА

ЖИВЕТ ГЕНІЙ ПРОСВѢТЛЯ-
ЯСЬ
ДЛЯ СИЛЬНЫХ И РЕТИВЫХ
УКОР
ГЕНІЯ ОТ СЕБЯ БРОСАЯ ЯСЬ
И ЕГО НЕИСЧИСЛЕН
ПРОСТОР

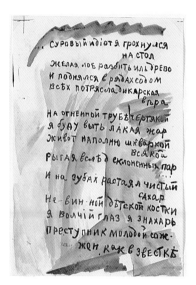

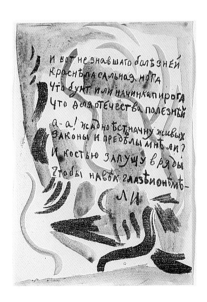

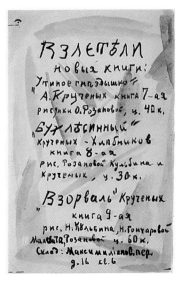

Olga V. Rozanova
Alexei E. Kruchenykh
Russian, 1886–1918 and 1885–1922

Universal War   1916
12 collages, approximately 8⅜ × 11¾ (22.2 × 29.8) each
Provenance: Bruner Gossweiler, Bern, Switzerland; Carus
Gallery, New York, 1984

Zaum principles, initially codified by a group of transrationalist poets led by Alexei Kruchenykh and Velimir Khlebnikov, deeply influenced Kazimir Malevich's development toward Suprematism and Olga Rozanova's nonobjective triumphs. Malevich synthesized Cubism, Futurism, and the transrational juxtapositions characteristic of *zaum* and subsequently composed an alogical, deconstructive/constructive system. In a like manner, Rozanova would integrate intuition, rhythm, color correlation, chance, and displacement into her own nonobjective work, of which the collages of *Universal War* are a primary example.

By 1915, Rozanova had begun to compose *zaum* poetry, but it was through her experimentation with nonobjective art that she contributed most effectively to the history of the early twentieth-century Russian avant-garde. At about this time, she executed her first fashion and embroidery designs, selections of which were later included in the proofs for *Supremus,* a Suprematist journal planned, but never published, by Malevich and his colleagues. In March of 1915, Rozanova participated in the "Tramway V" exhibition in Petrograd, where some of Vladimir Tatlin's early three-dimensional reliefs were shown. Rosanova's own abstract sculptures (now nonextant) were exhibited during the January 1916 "0.10 The Last Futurist Exhibition of Paintings" in Petrograd. Soon thereafter, Rozanova became affiliated with the newly formed Suprematist group and, while a member of the circle, realized some of her nonobjective masterpieces, for example, the collages included in *Universal War* of 1916.

Rozanova's discovery of the brilliant, nonobjective language through which she speaks so eloquently in the "Colored Cutouts" of the *Universal War* series can be traced to her visual experiments of 1913 and onwards. As was also the case with Malevich, her abstract triumphs were further facilitated through her affiliations with the *zaum* poets and her deep conviction of the universality of transrational principles. While it is true that Malevich and Rozanova influenced each other, it is also evident that each reached a conclusion independently of the other. In much the same way that the *zaum* poets broke common language down to a set of absolute, primary components, and recomposed these elements into private linguistic systems, Rozanova liberated pure color and form from all representational responsibility and recomposed these elements into a new expressive language that was both private and universal.

The preface to *Universal War,* a project completed in collaboration with Kruchenykh, stresses Rozanova's previous breakthroughs in nonobjective art. Issued in an edition of one hundred copies, the folio is composed of twelve pages of *zaum* text and twelve magnificent collages bearing the titles *Battle of the Futurist and the Ocean, Battle of Mars with Scorpio, Explosion in a Trunk, Wrestling with the Equator, Betrayal, Destructions of Gardens, The Battle Between India and Europe, Heavy Gun, Germany Arrogant, Germany Lying in Dust, Prayer for Victory,* and *Military State.* Unlike some of the earlier collaborations between the two, for example, *A Duck's Nest . . .* (1914), the text and images are no longer intertwined but rather are presented autonomously, conforming to equivalent principles yet maintaining their discrete boundaries. Purportedly based on Kruchenykh's belief that it was possible to calculate the periodicity of history, *Universal War* predicts the outbreak of interplanetary conflict in the year 1985. As suggested by the titles of some of the collages—for example, *Germany Arrogant* and *Germany Lying in Dust*—Kruchenykh and Rozanova also responded to some of the cataclysmic events of their own period of history even as they predicted the future. The collages are informed by concepts such as counterpoint and disjunction/conjunction as well as by the principles identified in Rozanova's 1913 manifesto, "The Basis of the New Creativity and the Reasons for Its Misinterpretation": "Volume equilibrium, weight and weightlessness . . . rhythm as a legitimate division of space, design, plane and surface dimension, texture, color correlation, and others" (Rozanova, 14–22). Perhaps even more important, the suite of color cutouts responds to the primary characteristic by which Rozanova believed the creative process to be informed, the "intuitive principle" through which one attains access to universal vision.

E.M.

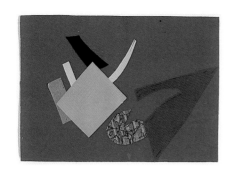

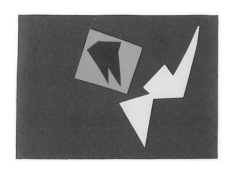
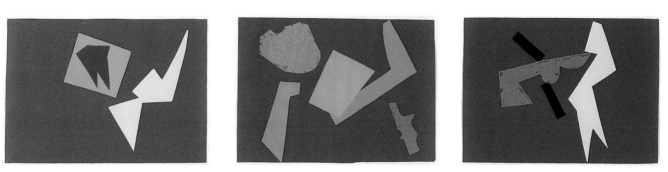
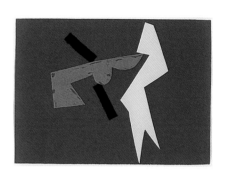

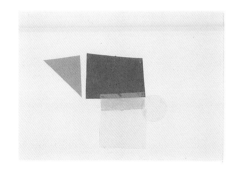

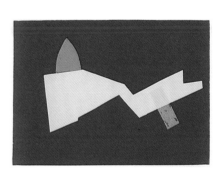

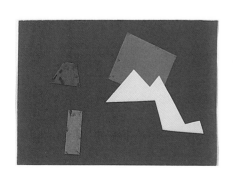
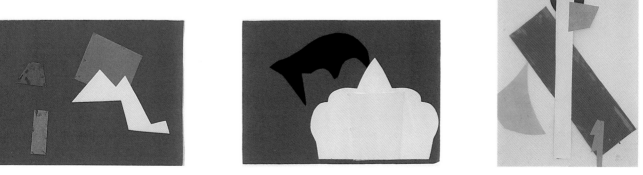

Cornelis Ruhtenberg

American, born in Latvia in 1923

Basket on Pink Ground   1987
Acrylic on Masonite, 19½ × 23½ (49.5 × 59.7)
Provenance: The artist, December 1987

Prior to emigrating to the United States in 1948, Cornelis Ruhtenberg was a resident of both Sweden and Germany. While living in Germany, she studied at the Hochschule für Bildende Kunst in Berlin from 1941 to 1946, worked with Karl Hofer and Max Kaus, and first exhibited her artwork. Throughout her career, her work has reflected her interests in the art of both northern Europe and the Far East. As a resident of Des Moines for the past twenty years, she has maintained an active professional life as a practicing artist and as a teacher of painting, participating in many national exhibitions and one-person shows of her paintings in New York City, and serving as an instructor of painting at Drake University and the Des Moines Art Center. Her work is represented in a number of collections, including that of the Hirshhorn Museum in Washington, D.C.

    Basket on Pink Ground is a study of subtle chromatic harmonies and of the act of composing, as well as of the objects it depicts. The low-keyed colors and serene, almost austere composition invite quiet contemplation of the objects themselves—two eggs in a wicker basket. The intricate basket is presented against the quietly modulated field of color, which itself has been framed by the artist's penciled margins. These marks perhaps restate the artist's primary concern with composition and, as they reframe the subject, suggest that this painting is an examination of the meanings to be disclosed by our close observation of objects, even such simple subjects as these two eggs and the basket that contains them.

J.S.

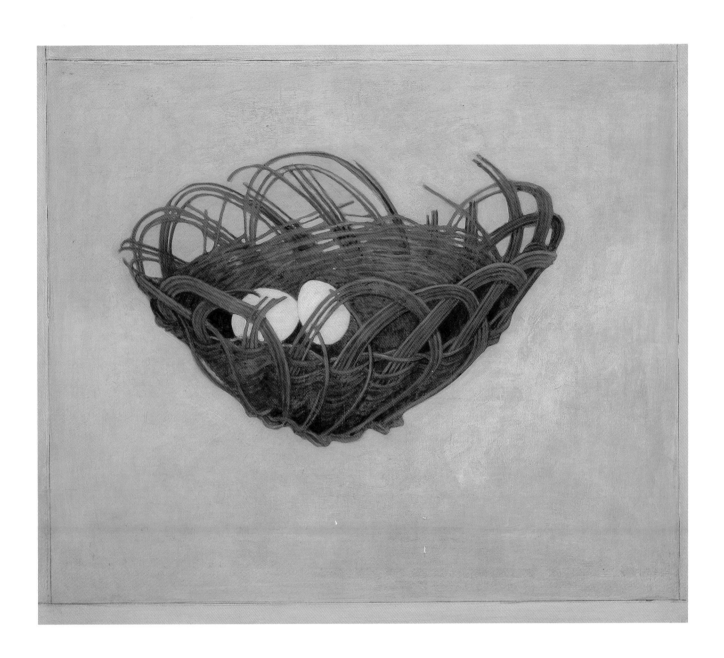

Anne Ryan

American, 1889–1954

Untitled (no. 588)   after 1948
Collage, 3⅝ × 3½ (9.2 × 8.9)
Provenance: Washburn Gallery, New York, 1989

Anne Ryan's collages address us on an intimate scale, quietly and richly. By exploiting the sensuous properties of diverse materials, and by making the process more deliberative—one senses an almost reverential attitude toward their selection and deployment—she extended collage into realms of pictorial experience hitherto unexplored. At the same time, through her fascination with the very substance of things, she retained a hold on collage's literal and physical past. It is at once remarkable and regrettable that only six years elapsed between her encounter with Schwitters' work and her death in 1954—the one because she achieved so much, the other because, having started so late, she was denied the opportunity of carrying it further. (Gibson, n.p.)

Eric Gibson's remarks, from the catalogue for a posthumous exhibition of Anne Ryan's collages, capture much of the special appeal of her work.

Born in Hoboken, New Jersey, in 1899, Ryan was married and a mother by the time she was twenty-two, and became a published writer—of *Lost Hills,* a book of poetry—by the time her youngest child was six. In the early thirties, she lived in Spain and spent a summer in Paris, where she saw and admired the art of Joan Miró. Returning to the United States, she lived in Greenwich Village and became a part of the vital artistic life centered there. Among her friends were Hans Hofmann, Tony Smith, and Barnett Newman.

In 1938, with Hofmann's encouragement, she began to paint and three years later had her first solo exhibition. She next studied printmaking in Stanley William Hayter's printmaking studio, Atelier XVII. It was only after 1948 that she turned to the work for which she is best remembered—collage. Ryan collage retrospectives have been held with regularity since her death in 1954.

The whimsy of Miró, or the color and structure of Hofmann, might be said to be reflected in Ryan's work. The greatest single influence upon her, however, was unquestionably that of Kurt Schwitters, whose work Ryan first saw in 1948. Captivated by an exhibition of Schwitters's collages, Ryan began to create the delicate, intimately scaled works of which the Noun collage is one.

Although at times Ryan's works depict highly abstracted figural subjects, the majority of her collages are nonobjective. Occasionally she incorporates words, or fragments of words, to signify a specific point of departure or meaning. Her use of fabric—especially that with a transparent gauzelike weave—is her distinctive innovation. Her exquisite sense of color results in works that range from delicate and monochromatic (like the Noun collage) to intense and vibrant to a precisely chosen full range of lights and darks, pales and brights. There is a wonderful duality in Ryan's collages between their apparent found-object nature—which gives them a sense of change and randomness—and the calculated deliberation with which they are composed.

Reviewers of Ryan's work have spoken of its "sensitive, lighter than air" quality and her "almost perfect control" (*Art News,* 51). Though it is hard to say whether Ryan would have wished to read one critic's remarks on her "wonderfully feminine understanding of materials and their use," that same reviewer also offered her the ultimate accolade: posterity "may someday assign her a position as secure as Kurt Schwitters'" (*Art Digest,* 21).

G.Z.

30/50

Nadezhda Andreevna Udaltsova

Russian, 1886–1961

Suprematist Composition   1916
Gouache, 12⅞ × 9½ (32.7 × 24.1)
Provenance: Galerie Gmurzynska, Cologne, 1984

Like Popova, Nadezhda Udaltsova studied Cubism at La
Palette, the studio of, most notably, Le Fauconnier and
Metzinger. Udaltsova participated in the 1914 Moscow ex-
hibition, "Jack of Diamonds," and in the winter of 1914–15
she also exhibited work in the Futurist show "Tramway V."
Although she had work in the 1915 Futurist exhibition
"0.10" in Petrograd, that same year she began to study
Suprematism. From 1916 through 1917 she was a member of
the group Supremus, which included Kazimir Malevich,
Vladimir Tatlin, Luibov Popova, and others.

Contrary to what its title suggests, Udaltsova's *Suprematist Composition* does not possess the typical elements one
expects from a follower of Malevich. At this time,
Udaltsova was still strongly committed to the use of a
Cubist vocabulary, manifested in the stacking of planes one
on top of another. Unlike many of her contemporaries she
considered herself primarily an easel painter, not a produc-
tionist (Drevina, 309). In 1921 she broke with Inkhuk, the
Institute of Artistic Culture, an organization which was
committed to pro-production art. Her advocacy of easel
painting distinguishes her from other artists, for example,
Kogan, who espoused both Malevich's ideology and vocabulary, and Stepanova, who believed in the artist's role as
social engineer. Udaltsova's *Suprematist Composition,* however, serves as an excellent example of the way in which
many Russian artists of the teens and twenties aligned
themselves with multiple movements.

                                        E.B.

Suzanne Valadon
(Marie Clémentine Valadon)
French, 1865–1938

Louise Nude on the Couch   1895
Soft ground etching, 9⅞ × 11¼ (25.1 × 28.6)
Provenance: M. Knoedler and Co., New York, 1975

Marie-Clémentine Valadon came with her mother from the provinces to Paris as a five-year-old illegitimate child. Going to work at a very early age, she supported herself as a milliner's apprentice, made funeral wreaths, sold vegetables, and worked as a waitress. She eventually joined the Mollier circus as an acrobat; Berthe Morisot drew her there as a tightrope artist. After a bad fall from a trapeze at the age of fifteen, Valadon looked for other jobs in her Montmartre neighborhood. She made many friends among the artists and others who frequented the dance halls and cabarets, and she began to work as a painter's model. At the age of eighteen she gave birth to a son, Maurice Utrillo. Among the artists for whom she frequently posed were Puvis de Chavannes, Renoir, Toulouse-Lautrec, Steinlen, and Forain. She also posed for many of the older academic artists, spurring Toulouse-Lautrec to give her the nickname Suzanne (after the biblical Suzanna and the Elders). Her adoption of the name was an acknowledgment of the voyeurism of the male artist with respect to the model. It also alluded to the fact that she, as a figure, was constantly being recreated by different artists to be what they wanted her to be. In order to establish her own identity, she herself had to draw and paint.

Valadon had drawn constantly since childhood. She never had any formal training, but her work as a model gave her the opportunity to study the work and procedures of many artists at close hand. After Renoir and Toulouse-Lautrec discovered her work, the sculptor Bartholomé urged her to bring her drawings to Degas, who admired them greatly. Valadon never modeled for Degas, but they became close friends. It was Degas who first bought Valadon's drawings. In 1894 he introduced her, in the only direct training she ever had, to soft ground etching. Degas had done experimental work with soft ground and aquatint as late as 1879–80, especially in his prints of Mary Cassatt at the Louvre. By this date, he was no longer making prints, because of his failing eyesight. However, his late prints—a lithograph of nude dancers and a series of a single nude drying herself, from 1891—relate to Valadon's nude studies at this time. Valadon printed her early soft ground etchings on Degas' press.

The line of a soft ground etching differs from the conventional etched line in that it appears to have been drawn with graphite. In *Louise Nude on the Couch,* Valadon either scribed through the resist into the metal or etched her plates so deeply that the printed lines belie the soft ground technique. Roger-Marx wrote of her technique:

> The artist has driven her line straight like a plowman; the acid seething in the furrows will enlarge them still further. Soft ground etching technicians excel with grays, pale golds, and half-tones. Here it is almost as if a sculptor had defined the planes, contrived the profiles and given so much weight to each form, in particular to the nudes which, although produced on white paper, have the gloss and hardness of marble. (Warnod, 55)

Valadon also combined drypoint with soft ground, and around 1904 she made traditional etchings as well. Ambroise Vollard published her first plates in *Le Revue et l'idée* and in the 1896 *Album des peintres graveurs* (Warnod, 55).

Valadon successfully transferred her astonishing command of line from drawing to etching, concentrating on images of solitary figures, stripped bare, in simply furnished rooms. In her prints, Valadon, herself a model to artists and a lover to many men, draws her own life. *Louise Nude on the Couch* depicts a nude female figure half reclining against a large couch with undulating woodwork and three huge pillows. Her head is averted and is seen from below. Her legs are spread apart, the left knee raised, in a gesture of exhaustion, as if after sex. She displays her body insistently, almost defiantly. The figure is drawn with a heavy, continuous, very sure outline.

A.W.

Suzanne Valadon
1895

Charmion von Wiegand
American, 1896–1983

Untitled   1957–66
Collage, 13 × 10⅛ (33.0 × 25.7)
Provenance: Marilyn Pearl Gallery, New York, 1985

In the 1930s, when Charmion von Wiegand's name first appears in the history of American art, the Western world was deep in economic depression and fascism was advancing across Europe. Artists in the United States debated the nature of a genuine American art: on the one hand, the Regionalist style of Grant Wood, Thomas Hart Benton, and John Steuart Curry had won popular acclaim; on the other, many artists and critics felt it depicted a mythical world unrelated to the realities of the time.

Von Wiegand entered this debate as a writer for *Art Front*, the periodical of the leftist Artists Union of New York City. Expressionism, she said in a 1936 review of work by the German artist Karl Schmidt-Rotluff, "seeks to break up the old forms, suffuses them in the brilliant colors of sunset, espouses the universal man against the petty individual, is *forward* moving. Its destructive activism is necessary in clearing the ground for future building" (von Wiegand, 1936, 10). She specifically rejected abstraction, saying a world in trouble couldn't wait for this new kind of art to "create new forms suitable for the new society" — the socialist society many artists then advocated.

Von Wiegand's own work as an artist was at this time a private undertaking. She had realized in the 1920s that her career as a writer was not wholly satisfying and had begun to study painting while continuing to write for *Art Front* and *New Masses* (the leftist journal whose cofounder, Joseph Freeman, she married in 1932). The daughter of Karl von Wiegand, an editor for Hearst newspapers, von Wiegand had lived and traveled in many countries, exploring Italian art and the archeology of Greece, Rome, Egypt, and Byzantium, working in Moscow for three years and venturing out to Georgia, the Ukraine, and Yalta on the strength of her "kitchen Russian" and her endless energy (Larsen, 29). Her art would thus be informed both by her changing environment and her wide-ranging studies. The titles of some of her works suggest their sources: *The Ka Door, City Lights, St. John the Baptist, The Pillars of Zen,* and *Chinese Theatre.*

Von Wiegand's ideas about abstraction underwent radical change in the early 1940s when she became a friend of the Dutch artist Piet Mondrian, recently arrived in New York. "From that first meeting," she said later, "my eyes were transformed. . . . I saw everything differently" (Rowell, 108). Intense study of his philosophical theory — Neo-Plasticism, which proposed an art based on such universal principles that it would bring all of life into a state of harmony — led her to a "historic role"; not only did she write the first American critical essay on Mondrian, but she turned the typical grid of Mondrian's style into the structure of her own original work (Frank, 110). Upon this grid she imposed her own color sense, which utilized the "naturalistic" green rejected by her mentor. By the late forties, she was exhibiting regularly, often with the American Abstract Artists.

Mondrian died in 1944, but his influence on von Wiegand's art lasted until 1959, when she painted a group of works she called "Hommages." At that time she turned to an intensive study — with her good friend Mark Tobey — of non-Western art and Tibetan Buddhism, traveling to Tibet to visit the Dalai Lama until she was in her eighties.

Von Wiegand began to make collages in the late 1940s and continued to do so throughout her long public career; they are among the most individual of her works. The Noun collage is composed of New York City bus transfers, which date to 1966, adhered to a 1957 work consisting of a board covered partially with watercolored fabric. It reflects at once her reverence for Mondrian's grid, her fascination with the city she lived in, and the energy and sense of humor that characterize the adventuresome life and artistic work of this unorthodox woman.

G.Z.

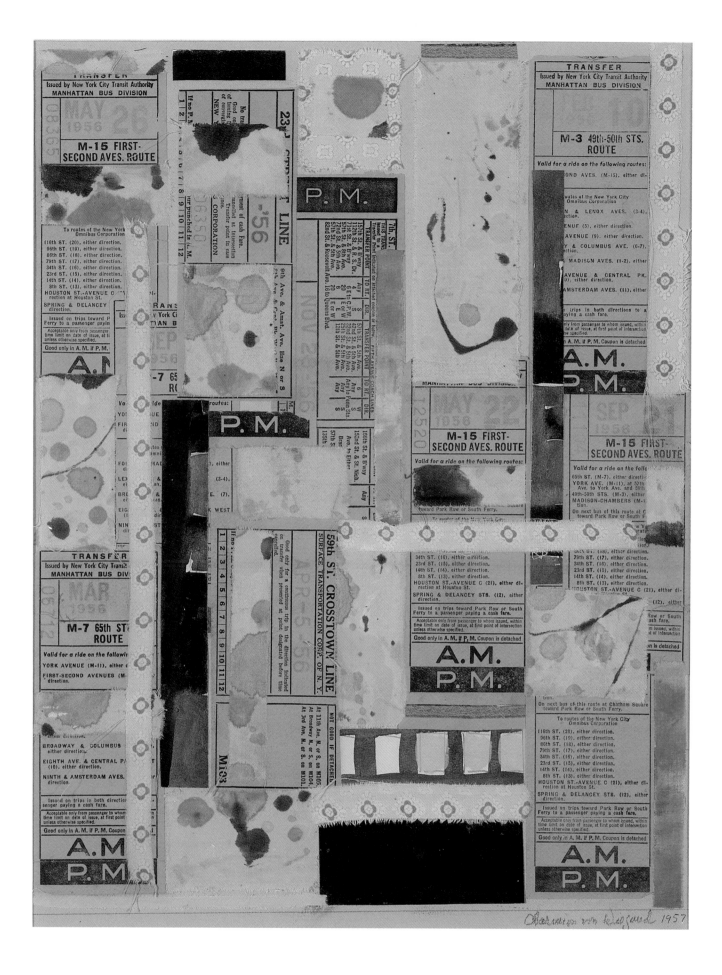

Amy Namowitz Worthen

American, born in 1946

Amy Worthen has pursued a form of visual expression that unites her interests in classical and contemporary architecture with her high regard for the tradition of printmaking. Concentrating on the oldest and most direct printmaking techniques, Worthen uses engraving and drypoint to enhance the strength of her perspectives and pictorial spaces. Much of the attraction of her work lies in the constant interplay between this strength and the subtleties of architectural details and often playful images.

Engravings like *Stairway with Skeleton* and *Senlis* explore forms and spaces that have made real and direct impressions on Worthen. Working from specific buildings, she constructs her images from numerous on-site drawings and then invests the whole with a sensitive draftsmanship and spatial complexity that invites close examination. In *Stairway with Skeleton,* based on the Iowa State Capitol, Worthen develops a visually delightful architectural setting and then lends an element of fantasy to the image by playfully including a skeleton that recalls the early inhabitants of the capitol. By her own account, the white marble of the stairway depicted in this print reminded Worthen of bones.

Senlis was engraved from pen and ink drawings of a church in Senlis, France, which Worthen visited in 1983, and is one in a series of six engravings of churches. The impression included in this exhibition was printed on marbled paper as a visual reminder of the marble that can be seen in old European churches. It is also an indication of Worthen's flexibility regarding materials, just as her architectural subjects reflect her broad interests in styles of regions as diverse as Iowa, Japan, France, Italy, Greece, and Germany.

Worthen studied printmaking with Leonard Baskin at Smith College and continued her work as a graduate student under Mauricio Lasansky at the University of Iowa. She received her M.A. in 1969 and has been living and printmaking in Des Moines since 1970. She has exhibited prints and drawings throughout Iowa and has fulfilled commissions for the Terrace Hill Society, the Weitz Corporation, and the Des Moines Metro Opera.

D.D.

10/ Stairway with Skeleton   Amy N. Worthen

Marguerite Thompson Zorach

American, 1887–1968

Jessie Bender 1913
Watercolor, 10½ × 8 (26.7 × 20.3)
Provenance: Tessim Zorach; Kraushaar Galleries, New
York, 1974

It may be considered anathema within a publication that celebrates the art of women to discuss the relationship of an artist to her artist husband, and certainly the work of Marguerite Thompson Zorach, one of the most renowned modernist artists working in New York in the second decade of the twentieth century, stands on its own. Zorach's works, among very few by women, were included in the historic modernist exhibits: the Armory Show of 1913, the "Forum Exhibition of Modern American Painters" in 1916, and the annual exhibitions of the Society of Independent Artists.

However, it is also true that Marguerite and William Zorach had an uncommon partnership. From 1911 to 1918, during their formative years as artists, their stylistic development ran parallel courses. They studied together in Paris, where they met in 1911 at La Palette (a progressive, nonacademic school), and after their marriage they shared the same artistic friends, attended and exhibited at the same shows, and painted in the same places. Following the birth of their children, Tessim in 1915 and Dahlov in 1917, they shared domestic duties, with one painting in the morning while the other tended to the children, and the other working in the afternoon. Zorach credited the ease with which she gained recognition to her relationship with William. Quoted in the *Christian Science Monitor* of April 12, 1926, upon the event of the first exhibition of the Society of Women Artists, of which she was president, she states that it was often difficult if not impossible for women artists to secure adequate exhibitions, and continues, "My husband and I held joint exhibitions for many years; we were a team, and dealers were not afraid of me. I am certain that had I been on my own I should not have enjoyed the freedom from practical annoyance which has been of untold benefit to me."

The works in the Noun Collection, executed in 1913, 1916, and 1917, stem from this period of parallel development, and from a period of artistic experimentation before each artist developed a mature style. In the late teens Zorach turned to fabric and tapestry design and her husband to sculpture. Although her tapestries were well received and exhibited, it has been suggested that her choice of a "women's medium" may have contributed to the fact that her artistic reputation was somewhat eclipsed by that of her husband in later years (Hoffman, 26).

Marguerite Thompson grew up in Fresno, California, and traveled to Paris in the fall of 1908. Attending the Salon d'Automne on the day of her arrival, she saw the work of the Fauves: Henri Matisse, André Derain, Albert Marquet, and John Duncan Fergusson (a Scot who was to become her teacher at La Palette). Her only other experience with "Post-Impressionism" (a term then used to include Fauves, Cubists, Futurists, Synchromists, Expressionists, and others) had been a visit to the Art Institute of Chicago en route to Paris. Immediately taken with the Fauves' non-realistic and expressive use of color, she allied herself to these artists, exhibiting with the Société des Artistes Indépendants and in the Salon d'Automne in 1911.

Thompson returned to the United States, moved to New York, and married William Zorach in December of 1912, arriving just two months before the Armory Show. In 1913 she executed several portraits of artists and friends, including the portrait of *Jessie Bender*. Each relies on judicial use of line, open spaces, and to one extent or another the expressive Fauvist color of her Paris training. Her contribution to the Armory Show was one such portrait, which remains unidentified, and which was harshly and sarcastically reviewed by a critic unsympathetic to modern art: "You see at once that the lady is feeling very, very bad. . . . The pale yellow eyes and the purple lips of her subject indicate that the digestive organs are not functioning properly. I would advise salicylate of quinine in small doses" (Tarbell, 1973, 36). The portrait of *Jessie Bender* is more conventional but shares the general characteristics of her other portraits. Jessie was the daughter of a destitute family William had roomed with when he first came to New York in 1908. An "enchanting little black-eyed, black-haired sprite" (Zorach, 15), she would have been twelve years old when Zorach painted this portrait.

J.C.

Jessie Bender.

M. ZORACH
-1913-

Marguerite Thompson Zorach

American, 1887–1968

TOP:
Provincetown Players   circa 1916
Linocut, 7¾ × 11⅝ (19.7 × 29.5)
Provenance: Weyhe Gallery, New York

BOTTOM:
Forest Edge   1917
Watercolor, 10⅝ × 13⅝ (27.0 × 34.6) (sight)
Provenance: Kraushaar Galleries, New York, 1966

Marguerite and William Zorach agreed to live in New York, believing that the greatest opportunities for artists were to be found there. However, Marguerite preferred rural areas. As a compromise they decided to leave the city every summer, and over the years they summered in various parts of New England: Chappaqua, New York; Randolph and Plainfield, New Hampshire; Provincetown, Massachusetts; and Stoningham, Maine. It was during these summer respites that Zorach produced most of her works.

In 1916 the Zorachs traveled to Provincetown, where William was supposed to teach. Then, as now, many artists gathered in Provincetown in the summer. No students enrolled in William's class, but the Zorachs stayed on and became involved with the Provincetown Players. A group of then little-known writers, the company was the first to produce the plays of Eugene O'Neill. For the next five years, the Zorachs designed and painted scenery for plays by Eugene O'Neill, Louise Bryant, Edna St. Vincent Millay, Alfred Kreymborg, and others.

Zorach's linoleum cut *Provincetown Players* is thought to have been made that first summer in Provincetown. She had had some experience in printmaking, having executed etchings and linocuts while in Paris, and during this summer she worked with B. J. O. Nordfeldt on relief prints. (Nordfeldt is credited with inventing the "Provincetown print," a single-block color woodcut process.) Stylistically the print is closer to Zorach's tapestries and fabric designs, which stressed dynamic formal composition and incorporated arcadian and primitive elements, than to her oils from this period, which show, alternately, the influence of Cubism (utilizing multiple simultaneous viewpoints) and Synchromism (utilizing curved abstract forms and bright colors).

The years 1915–18 have been called Zorach's Cubist period. Although she had viewed Picasso's Cubist works in Paris, at the residence of Leo and Gertrude Stein, it was not until 1914 that she began to incorporate Cubism into her work. Her Cubist experiments are most fully developed in oil paintings. In *Forest's Edge* and other watercolors from this period, she combines flattened geometric planes derived from her Cubist studies with a retained interest in expressive color. This combination of Fauve and Cubist elements would continue in works done after 1920.

The Zorachs spent the summer of 1917 in the White Mountains of New Hampshire. Marguerite found inspiration in mountains: a quotation from John Muir that made reference to the stimulating quality of mountains hung in her room in Paris, and her first major series of oils was done in the Sierra Mountains, just after her return from Paris. The Zorachs lived at Echo Farm, an abandoned property near Plainfield, which was lent to them by a friend, and it was here that Zorach executed *Forest's Edge*. William described the summer as idyllic, even though he was having difficulty painting. "Marguerite [on the other hand] did a series of watercolors of the woods, pictures that analyzed the colors and forms around her and built them into new combinations, yet retained the beauty of the woods" (Zorach, 49).

J.C.

Bibliography

General

Bowlt, John E. *Russian Art 1875–1975*. New York: MSS Information Corporation, 1976.

————, ed. and trans. *Russian Art of the Avant-Garde: Theory and Criticism 1902–1934*. Rev. ed. New York: Thames and Hudson, 1988.

————. *The Silver Age: Russian Art of the Early Twentieth Century and the "World of Art" Group*. Newtonville, MA: Oriental Research Partners, 1979.

Broude, Norma, and Mary D. Garrad, eds. *Feminism and Art History: Questioning the Litany*. New York: Harper and Row, 1982.

Fine, Elsa Honig. *Women and Art: A History of Women Painters and Sculptors from the Renaissance to the Twentieth Century*. Montclair and London: Allanheld and Schram/Prior, 1978.

Gabhart, Ann, and Elizabeth Broun. "Old Mistresses: Women Artists of the Past." *Bulletin of the Walters Art Gallery* 24 (April 1972): n.p.

Galerie Gmurzynska. *Women-Artists of the Russian Avantgarde 1910–1930*. Cologne: Galerie Gmurzynska, 1979.

————. *Seven Moscow Artists 1910–1930*. Cologne: Galerie Gmurzynska, 1984.

Garrard, Mary D. " 'Of Men, Women and Art': Some Historical Reflections." *Art Journal* 35 (Summer 1976): 324–29.

Gornick, Vivian, and Barbara K. Moran. *Women in Sexist Society: Studies in Power and Powerlessness*. New York and London: Basic Books, 1971.

Gouma-Peterson, Thalia, and Patricia Matthews. "The Feminist Critique of Art History." *Art Bulletin* 69 (September 1987): 326–57. See also the discussion by Norma Broude and Mary P. Garrard and the reply by Gouma-Peterson and Matthews, *Art Bulletin* 71 (March 1989): 124–27.

Gray, Camilla. *The Russian Experiment in Art, 1863–1922*. Rev. by Marian Burleigh-Motley. London: Thames and Hudson, 1986.

Harris, Ann Sutherland, and Linda Nochlin. *Women Artists: 1550–1950*. New York and Los Angeles: Alfred A. Knopf and the Los Angeles County Museum of Art, 1976.

Heller, Nancy G. *Women Artists: An Illustrated History*. New York: Abbeville Press, 1982.

Krasilovsky, Alexis Rafael. "Feminism in the Arts: An Interim Bibliography." *Artforum* 10 (June 1972): 76–78.

Lippard, Lucy R. *From the Center: Feminist Essays on Women's Art*. New York: E. P. Dutton, 1976.

————. *Issue: Social Strategies by Women Artists*. London: Institute of Contemporary Art, 1980.

————. *Overlay: Contemporary Art and the Art of Prehistory*. New York: Pantheon Books, 1983.

————. "Projecting a Feminist Criticism." *Art Journal* 35 (Summer 1976): 337–39.

Munro, Eleanor. *Originals: American Women Artists*. New York: Simon and Schuster, 1979.

Nesmer, Cindy. "Stereotypes and Women Artists." *Feminist Art Journal* 1 (April 1972): 1, 20–21.

Parker, Rozsika, and Griselda Pollock. *Old Mistresses: Women, Art and Ideology*. New York: Pantheon Books, 1981.

Petersen, Karen, and J. J. Wilson. *Women Artists: Recognition and Reappraisal. From the Early Middle Ages to the Twentieth Century*. New York: New York University Press, 1976.

Rudenstine, Angelica Zander, ed. *The George Costakis Collection: Russian Avant-garde Art*. New York: Harry N. Abrams, 1981.

Schwarz, Therese. "They Built Women a Bad Art History." *Feminist Art Journal* 2 (Fall 1973): 10–11, 22.

Vogel, Lisa. "Erotica, the Academy, and Art Publishing: A Review of *Woman as Sex Object: Studies in Erotic Art, 1730–1970*, New York 1972." *Art Journal* 35 (Summer 1976): 378–85.

White, Barbara Erlich. "A 1974 Perspective: Why Women's Studies in Art and Art History?" *Art Journal* 35 (Summer 1976): 340–44.

Withers, Josephine. "Artistic Women and Women Artists." *Art Journal* 35 (Summer 1976): 330–36.

Ella Bergmann

Campbell, Lawrence. "Ella Bergmann." *Arts Magazine* 109: 1 (September 1984): 16.

Chanin, A. L., and Herta Wescher. *Ella Bergmann + Robert Michel: Collagen, Zeichnungen 1917–1966.* Cologne: Galerie Bargera, 1974.

Herbert, Robert L., Eleanor S. Apter, and Elise K. Kenney. *The Société Anonyme and the Dreier Bequest at Yale University: A Catalogue Raisonné.* New Haven and London: Yale University Press, 1984.

Isabel Bishop

Alloway, Lawrence. "Isabel Bishop, the Grand Manner and the Working Girl." *Art in America* 63 (September–October 1975): 61–65.

Bishop, Isabel. "Concerning Edges." *Magazine of Art* 38 (May 1945): 168–73.

———. "Isabel Bishop Discusses Genre Drawings." *American Artist* 17 (Summer 1953): 46–47.

———. "Drawing the Nude." *Art in America* 60 (December 1963): 117.

Harms, Ernest. "Light is the Beginning—The Art of Isabel Bishop." *American Artist* 25 (February 1961): 28–33, 60–62.

Johnson, Una E. *Isabel Bishop: Prints and Drawings 1925–1964.* Brooklyn, NY: Brooklyn Museum, 1964.

Lunde, Karl. *Isabel Bishop.* New York: Harry N. Abrams, 1975.

Munro, Eleanor. *Originals: American Women Artists.* New York: Simon and Schuster, 1979, 145–53.

Reich, Sheldon. *Isabel Bishop.* Tucson: University of Arizona Museum of Art, 1974.

Seckler, Dorothy. "Bishop Paints a Picture." *Art News* 50 (November 1951): 38–41.

Louise Bourgeois

Bloch, Susi. "An Interview with Louise Bourgeois." *Art Journal* 35 (Summer 1976): 370–73.

Curtis, Cathy. "Louise Bourgeois: Blending Emotive Dualities." *Artweek* 14 (October 1, 1983): 1, 16.

Gorovoy, Jerry. *The Iconography of Louise Bourgeois.* New York: Max Hutchinson Gallery, 1980.

Kirili, Alain. "The Passion for Sculpture: A Conversation with Louise Bourgeois." *Arts Magazine* 63 (March 1989), 69–75.

Lippard, Lucy. *From the Center: Feminist Essays on Women's Art,* 238–49. New York: Dutton, 1976.

Louise Bourgeois: femme maison. Chicago: Renaissance Society, University of Chicago, 1981.

Munro, Eleanor. *Originals: American Women Artists.* New York: Simon and Schuster, 1979, 154–69.

Pincus-Witten, Robert. *Louise Bourgeois: Bourgeois Truth.* New York: Robert Miller Gallery, 1982.

Rubin, William. "Some Reflections Prompted by Recent Work of Louise Bourgeois." *Art International* 8 (April 1969): 17–20.

Swenson, Sally S. "Louise Bourgeois." In Lynn F. Miller and Sally S. Swenson, *Lives and Works: Talks with Women Artists.* Metuchen, NJ, and London: Scarecrow Press, 1981, 2–14.

Wye, Deborah. *Louise Bourgeois. A Retrospective.* New York: Museum of Modern Art, 1982.

Leonora Carrington

Billeter, Erika, and José Pierre. Preface by André Pieyre de Mandiargues. *La Femme et le surréalisme.* Lausanne: Musée cantonal des beaux-arts, 1987.

Carrington, Leonora. *The House of Fear, Notes from Down Below.* Intro. by Marina Warner. Trans. by Kathrine Talbot and Marina Warner. New York: E. P. Dutton, 1988.

Chadwick, Whitney. *Women Artists and the Surrealist Movement.* Over Wallop, NH: Thames and Hudson, 1985.

Orenstein, Gloria. "Leonora Carrington: Another Reality." *Ms.* 3 (August 1974): 27–31.

———. "Leonora Carrington: Visionary Artist for the New Age." *Chrysalis* 3 (1978): 65–77.

Ponce, Juan Garcia, and Leonora Carrington. *Leonora Carrington.* Mexico City: Ediciones Era, 1974.

Sonia Delaunay-Terk

Buck, Robert T., Sherry A. Buckberrough, and Susan Krane. *Sonia Delaunay: A Retrospective.* Buffalo: The Buffalo Fine Arts Academy, 1980.

Cohen, Arthur A. *Sonia Delaunay.* New York: Harry N. Abrams, 1975.

Delaunay und Deutschland. Cologne: Du Mont Buchverlag, 1985.

Dorival, Bernard. *Sonia Delaunay: sa vie et sa oeuvre.* Paris: J. Demase, 1980.

Galerie Gmurzynska. *Women-Artists of the Russian Avant-garde 1910-1930.* Cologne: Galerie Gmurzynska, 1979.

Alexandra Alexandrovna Exter

Bowlt, John E. "The Marionettes of Alexandra Exter." *Russian History/Histoire Russe* 8 (1981): 219-32. Also published in *Alexandra Exter, Marionettes.* New York: Leonard Hutton Galleries, 1975.

Marcarde, Jean-Claude. "Alexandra Exter or the Search for the Rhythms of Light-Colour." Trans. by A. J. Jordan. In Galerie Gmurzynska, *Women-Artists of the Russian Avantgarde 1910—1930.* Cologne: Galerie Gmurzynska, 1979, 125-28.

Nakov, Andrei B. *Alexandra Exter.* Paris: Galerie Jean Chauvelin, May-June 1972.

Natalia Sergeevna Gontcharova

Bowlt, John E. *Russian Art of the Avant-Garde: Theory and Criticism 1902-1934.* Rev. ed. New York: Thames and Hudson, 1988.

Chamot, Mary. "The Early Work of Goncharova and Larionov." *Burlington Magazine* 97 (June 1955): 170-74.

Retrospective. Larionov Gontcharova. Brussels: Musée d'Ixelles, 1976.

Musée Toulouse-Lautrec. *Michel Larionov et son temps.* Albi, France: Musée Toulouse-Lautrec, 1973.

Orenstein, Gloria. "Natalia Goncharova: Profile of the Artist—Futurist Style." *Feminist Art Journal* 3 (Summer 1974): 1, 3-6, 19.

Gertrude Greene

Kuntz, Margaret A. "Gertrude Greene." In *Beyond the Plane,* ed. Jennifer Toher. Trenton: New Jersey State Museum, 1983, 53-54.

Marter, Joan. "Beyond the Plane: American Constructions, 1930-1965." In *Beyond the Plane,* ed. Jennifer Toher. Trenton: New Jersey State Museum, 1983, 7-20.

Moss, Jacqueline. "Gertrude Greene: Constructions of the 1930s and 1940s." *Arts Magazine* 55 (April 1981): 120-27.

Florence Henri

Fabre, Gladys C., Barbara Rose, and Marie-Odile Broit. *Léger and the Modern Spirit: An Avant-garde Alternative to Non-Objective Art (1918-1931).* Paris: Musée d'art moderne de la ville de Paris, 1982.

De Miro d'Ajeta, Ester Carla. *Florence Henri.* Genoa and New York: Martini and Ronchetti, 1974.

Du Pont, Diana. Unpublished exhibition prospectus for "Florence Henri: Artist-Photographer of the Avant-Garde." San Francisco: San Francisco Museum of Modern Art, 1989.

Florence Henri. Genoa and New York: Martini and Ronchetti, 1974.

Molderings, Herbert. *Florence Henri: Aspekte der Photographie der Zwanziger Jahre.* Baden-Baden: Westfälischer Kunst-verein Münster/Staatliche Kunsthalle Baden-Baden, 1976.

Stein, Donna. *Towards the "Restructuring of the Universe."* New York: Rachel Adler Gallery, 1986.

Teicher, Hendel. *Florence Henri. Soixante-dix Photographies 1928-1938.* Geneva: Association musée d'art moderne, 1981.

Eva Hesse

Barrette, Bill. *Eva Hesse: Sculpture. Catalogue Raisonné.* New York: Timken Publishers, 1989.

Johnson, Ellen H. *Eva Hesse: A Retrospective of the Drawings.* Oberlin, OH: Allen Memorial Art Museum, 1982.

Lippard, Lucy. *Eva Hesse.* New York: New York University Press, 1976.

Pincus-Witten, Robert. "Eva Hesse: Post-Minimalism into Sublime." *Artforum* 10 (November 1971): 32-44.

Hannah Höch

Dech, Gertrud J. *Schnitt mit dem Küchenmesser DADA durch die letzte weimarer Bierbauchkulturepoche Deutschlands: Untersuchungen zur Fotomontage bei Hannah Höch.* Münster: Lit-Verlag, 1981.

Galerie Nierendorf. *Hannah Höch.* Berlin: Galerie Nierendorf, 1964.

————. *Hannah Höch.* Berlin: Galerie Nierendorf, 1975.

Adriani, Gotz, ed. *Hannah Höch: Fotomontagen, Gemälde, Aquarellen.* Cologne: Du Mont Buchverlag, 1980.

Karsch, Florian. *Gemälde, Collagen, Aquarellen, Zeichnungen. Hannah Höch zum neunzigsten Geburtstag.* Berlin: Galerie Nierendorf, 1979.

Lorenz, Marianne. "Hannah Höch's Dada Photomontages: An Iconography of the Berlin Years." M.A. thesis, University of Colorado, 1981.

Maurer, Ellen. "Symbolische Gemälde von Hannah Höch aus den Jahren 1920–1930." M.A. thesis, Ludwig-Maximilian-Universität, Munich, 1983.

Musée de l'art moderne de la ville de Paris and Nationalgalerie Berlin. *Hannah Höch: collages, peintures, aquarelles, gouaches, dessins.* Paris and Berlin: Musée de l'art moderne de la ville de Paris and Nationalgalerie Berlin, 1976.

Ohff, Heinz. *Hannah Höch.* Berlin: Gebrüder Mann, 1968.

Pierre, José. "Hannah Höch et photomontage des Dadaistes berlinois." *Apeiros* 6 (1974): 58–61.

Richter, Hans. *Dada Art and Anti-Art.* New York and Toronto: McGraw-Hill, 1964.

Roditi, Edouard. "Interview with Hannah Höch." *Arts* (December 1959): 24–29.

Wingler, Hans M. *The Bauhaus, Weimar, Dessau, Berlin, Chicago.* Cambridge, MA, and London: MIT Press, 1969.

Gwen John

Bass, Ruth. "New York Reviews: Gwen John, Davis and Langdale." *Art News* 84: 1 (January 1985): 148.

Chitty, Susan. *Gwen John.* New York: Franklin Watts, 1987.

Langdale, Cecily. *Gwen John: With a Catalogue Raisonné of the Paintings and a Selection of the Drawings.* New Haven and London: Yale University Press, 1987.

Langdale, Cecily, and David Fraser-Jenkins. *Gwen John: An Interior Life.* London: Barbican Art Gallery, 1985.

Taubman, Mary. *Gwen John.* London: Scolar Press, 1985.

Frida Kahlo (Magdelena Carmen Frida Kahlo y Calderón)

Herrera, Hayden. *Frida: A Biography of Frida Kahlo.* New York: Harper and Row, 1983.

Orenstein, Gloria. "Frida Kahlo: Painting for Miracles." *Feminist Art Journal* 2 (Fall 1973): 7–9.

Erika Giovanna Klien

Herbert, Robert L., Eleanor S. Apter, and Elise K. Kenney. *The Société Anonyme and the Dreier Bequest at Yale University: A Catalogue Raisonné.* New Haven and London: Yale University Press, 1984.

Vergine, Lea. *L'Altra Meta dell' Avanguardia 1910–1940.* Milan: Comune di Milano-Ripartizione Cultura, Gabriele Mazzotta editore, 1980.

Nina Osipovna Kogan

Bowlt, John E. "Malevich and His Students." *Soviet Union / Union Sovietique* 5 (1978): 256–86.

Kogan, Nina. "On the Graphics of the Unovis Programme." Unovis leaflet of the Vitebsk Art Committee, no. 1, November 20, 1920. Trans. Günter Hanne and A. J. Jordan. In Galerie Gmurzynska, *Women-Artists of the Russian Avantgarde 1910–1930.* Cologne: Galerie Gmurzynska, 1979, 163.

Käthe Schmidt Kollwitz

Bittner, Herbert. *Käthe Kollwitz Drawings.* New York and London: Thomas Yoseloff, 1959.

Kearns, Martha. *Käthe Kollwitz: Woman and Artist.* Old Westbury, NY: Feminist Press, 1976.

Klipstein, August. *Käthe Kollwitz. Verzeichnis des graphischen Werkes . . . für die Jahre 1890–1912 unter Verwendung des 1913 erschienen Oeuvrekataloges von Prof. Dr. Johannes Sievers.* Bern: Klipstein, 1955.

Kollwitz, Hans, ed. *The Diary and Letters of Käthe Kollwitz.* Trans. Richard and Clara Winston. Evanston, IL: Northwestern University Press, 1988.

Wagner, A. *Die Radierungen, Holzschnitten und Lithographien von Käthe Kollwitz: eine Zusammenstellung der seit 1912 entstandenen graphischen Arbeiten.* Dresden: Emil Richter, 1927.

Zigrosser, Carl. *Käthe Kollwitz.* New York: H. Bittner, 1946.

Lee Krasner (Lenore Krassner)

Lee Krasner: Collages. New York: Robert Miller Gallery, 1986.

Munro, Eleanor. *Originals: American Women Artists* (New York: Simon and Schuster, 1979), 100–119.

Rose, Barbara. *Lee Krasner: A Retrospective.* Houston and New York: Museum of Fine Arts and the Museum of Modern Art, 1983.

Lois Lane

Cecil, Sarah. "Lois Lane at Willard." *Art News* 84 (September 1985): 137.

Cohen, Ronny, and Melinda Wortz. "New Editions." *Art News* 81 (April 1982): 102 + .

Henry, Gerrit. "Lois Lane, Willard Gallery." *Art News* 82 (April 1983): 155.

Museum of Fine Arts. *The Modern Art of the Print: Selections from the Collection of Lois and Michael Torf.* Boston: Museum of Fine Arts, 1984.

Edith Lawrence

Lawrence, Edith, and Claude Flight. *A Little About Art.* London: Pittman and Son, 1938.

Parkin, Michael. *Claude Flight and His Circle.* London: Michael Parkin Fine Art, 1975.

—————, and Bernard Denvir. *Claude Flight and Edith Lawrence.* London: Michael Parkin Fine Art, 1973.

Urbanelli, Lora S. *The Grosvenor School: British Linocuts Between the Wars.* Providence: Museum of Fine Art, Rhode Island School of Design, 1988.

Blanche Lazzell

Campbell, Lawrence. "Blanche Lazzell at Martin Diamond Fine Arts." *Art in America* 74 (July 1986): 122–23.

Clarkson, John. *Blanche Lazzell.* Morgantown: Creative Art Century, West Virginia University, 1979.

Evual, William H. "The Provincetown Printers: Genesis of a Unique Color-Woodcut Process." *Print Review* 18 (1983): 57–66.

Flint, Janet Altic. *Provincetown Printers: A Woodcut Tradition.* Washington, D.C.: Smithsonian Institution Press, 1983.

Fort, Ilene Susan. "Blanche Lazzell." *Arts* 57 (October 1982): 20–21.

Marks, Matthew. "Provincetown Prints." *Print Collector's Newsletter* 15: 4 (September/October 1984): 131–33.

Agnes Martin

Alloway, Lawrence. *Agnes Martin.* Reprint of 1973 catalogue. Foreword by Suzanne Delahanty. Oral and written statements by Agnes Martin as recorded by Ann Wilson. Philadelphia: Institute of Contemporary Art, University of Pennsylvania, 1976.

Ashton, Dore. *Agnes Martin: Paintings and Drawings 1957–1975.* London: Arts Council of Great Britain, 1977.

Barron, Stephanie. "Giving Art History the Slip." *Art in America* 62 (March/April 1974): 80–84.

Borden, Lizzie. "Agnes Martin: Early Work." *Artforum* 11 (April 1973): 39–44.

Linville, Kasha. "Agnes Martin: An Appreciation." *Artforum* 9 (June 1971): 72–73.

Ada Medina

Awards in the Visual Arts 2. Chicago and Winston-Salem: Museum of Contemporary Art, Chicago, and the Southeastern Center for Contemporary Art, Winston-Salem, 1983.

Paula Modersohn-Becker

Blocher, Heidi. "On Paula Modersohn-Becker." *Womanart* 1 (Spring–Summer 1977): 13–17.

Busch, Günther, and Liselotte von Reinken. *Paula Modersohn-Becker. The Letters and Journals.* Ed. and trans. Arthur Wensinger and Carol Clew Hoey. New York: Taplinger Publishing Company, 1983.

Davidson, Martha. "Paula Modersohn-Becker: Struggle Between Life and Art." *Feminist Art Journal* 2 (Winter 1973–74): 1, 3–5.

Meyers, Bernard S. *The German Expressionists: A Generation in Revolt.* New York and Washington: Frederick A. Praeger, Publishers, 1966.

Modersohn-Becker, Paula. *The Letters and Journals of Paula Modersohn-Becker.* Trans. and annotated J. Diane Radycki. Metuchen, NJ: Scarecrow Press, 1980.

Oppler, Ellen C. "Paula Modersohn-Becker: Some Facts and Legends." *Art Journal* 35: 364–69.

Paula Modersohn-Becker, 1876–1907. Gemälde, Aquarellen, Zeichnungen, Druckgraphik. Bremen: Graphisches Kabinett, 1980.

Pauli, Gustav. *Paula Modersohn-Becker.* Leipzig: Kurt Wolff Verlag, 1922.

Perry, Gillian. *Paula Modersohn-Becker. Her Life and Work.* New York: Icon Editions, 1979.

Stelzer, Otto. *Paula Modersohn-Becker.* Berlin: Rembrandt-Verlag, 1958.

Berthe Morisot

Bailly-Herzberg, Janine. "Les Estampes de Berthe Morisot." *Gazette des Beaux-Arts,* ser. 6, 93 (May–June 1979): 223, no. 8.

Johnson, Una E. *Ambroise Vollard, Editeur.* New York: Museum of Modern Art, 1977.

Mongan, Elizabeth. *Berthe Morisot: Drawings, Pastels, Watercolors, Paintings.* New York: Tudor Publishing Co., 1960.

Nochlin, Linda. "Morisot's *Wet Nurse."* In *Women, Art, and Power.* New York: Harper and Row, 1988.

Passeron, Roger. *Impressionist Prints.* New York: Dutton, 1974.

Stuckey, Charles F., and William P. Scott. *Berthe Morisot: Impressionist.* New York: Hudson Hills Press, 1987.

Gabriele Münter

Comini, Alessandra. "State of the Field 1980: The Women Artists of German Expressionism." *Arts Magazine* 55 (November 1980): 147–53.

Erlanger, Liselotte. "Gabriele Münter: A Lesser Life?" *Feminist Art Journal* 3 (Winter 1974–75): 11–13, 23.

Gregg, Sara Helen. "The Art of Gabrielle Münter: An Evaluation of Content." M.A. thesis. State University of New York at Binghamton, 1980.

———. "Gabriele Münter in Sweden: Interlude and Separation." *Arts Magazine* 55 (May 1981): 116–19.

Helms, Sabine. *Gabriele Münter. Das Druckgraphische Werk.* Munich: Städtische Galerie im Lenbachhaus München, 1967.

Jacob, Mary Jane. *Naive and Outsider Painting from Germany, and Paintings by Gabriele Münter.* Chicago and New Haven: Museum of Contemporary Art and Eastern Press, 1983.

Lindsay, Kenneth. "Gabriele Münter and Wassily Kandinsky: What They Meant to Each Other." *Arts Magazine* 56 (December 1981): 56–62.

Meyers, Bernard S. *The German Expressionists. A Generation in Revolt.* New York, Toronto, London: McGraw-Hill Book Company, 1963.

Mochon, Anne. Gabriele Münter. *Between Munich and Murnau.* Cambridge: Busch-Reisinger Museum, Harvard University, 1980.

Gabriele Münter. Laguna Beach, CA: Laguna Beach Museum of Art, 1978.

Roditi, Edouard. "Interview with Gabriele Münter." *Arts* (January 1960): 36–41.

Spalek, John M., Bruce M. Broerman, Carol L. Paul, and Henry A. Smith III. *German Expressionism in the Fine Arts. A Bibliography.* Los Angeles: Hennessey and Ingalls, 1977.

Terenzio, Stephanie. "Gabriele Münter in 1908." *William Benton Museum of Art Bulletin.* Storrs: University of Connecticut, 1974, 3-17.

Agnes Pelton

"Calendar of Exhibitions in New York: Agnes Pelton, Contemporary Modernist, Argent Galleries." *Art News* 29: 1 (February 21, 1931): 10.

Opitz, Glenn B., ed. *Mantle Fielding's Dictionary of American Painters, Sculptors, and Engravers.* 2d. ed. Poughkeepsie, NY: Apollo, 1986.

Tufts, Eleanor, Gail Levin, Alessandra Comini, and Wanda M. Korn. *American Women Artists 1830–1930.* Washington, D.C.: National Museum of Women in the Arts, 1987.